COME THOU AND WALK WITH ME

*A Collection
of Ray's Writings
on his Walks
with God*

RAY BROWN

Come Thou and Walk with Me

*A Collection
of Ray's Writings
on his Walks
with God*

Ray Brown

VisionRun
PUBLISHING

Come Thou and Walk with Me,
A Collection of Ray's Writings on his Walks with God
by Ray Brown

ISBN 978-1-954509-11-5

Scriptures marked NLT are taken from the HOLY BIBLE, NEW LIVING TRANSLATION (NLT): Scriptures taken from the HOLY BIBLE, NEW LIVING TRANSLATION, Copyright© 1996, 2004, 2007 by Tyndale House Foundation. Used by permission of Tyndale House Publishers, Inc., Carol Stream, Illinois 60188. All rights reserved. Used by permission.

Scriptures used are taken from the Holy Bible, KING JAMES VERSION, which is in the public domain.

Seaside Sunrise photo by Kathy Garvey
Abide in Me photo by Beverly Baker
Gift of Light photo by Mark Brown
All other photography by Ray Brown

Printed in the United States
visionrun.com

*With love, dedication, and thanks to the Lord Jesus Christ,
my wife Ethel, and the many friends in the family of God who
have encouraged my walk with Him.*

Ray Brown

Contents

Introduction

In writing this book I owe loving gratitude to my family and many friends, who encouraged me to assemble in book form the many inspirations the Holy Spirit has prompted me to share. I am also thankful to be able to work with Debbie Patrick, my friend and editor, without her this book would not have been possible. Much of my writing has occurred spontaneously when touched by meditating on events occurring in nature. A portion of my writing is personification of objects that portray a spiritual truth. Walking is one of my pleasures and being sensitive to natural surroundings to discover a spiritual lesson is my motivation. Some of the writings are memories, as I recall subjects and events that have made an impression on my life.

My purpose in writing this book is to glorify God, and to impart his life-changing truths to all who read it. The book also reveals how Jesus has changed my life in recent years to consider the heavenly unseen rather than concentrate on the worldly temporal sights.

This book which I entitled *Come Thou And Walk With Me* express the fact that I love to walk with Jesus. The title was taken from a phrase in a gospel song and a happening that touched my heart. The happening occurred while I was working the polls during early voting. A wheelchair-bound gentleman approached my station wearing a cap which had "Walk with Jesus" printed on the front. I teasingly told him I would like to steal his cap. When he finished voting he returned to my table and said I want to give you my cap. I tried to refuse it, but he insisted I take his cap, so I did. The irony of this story was a man who couldn't walk and loved Jesus gave his cap to someone who could walk and also loves Jesus. This became a confirmation to me that I was to continue walking and especially in the presence of Jesus.

Jesus said come thou and walk with me, the cap said walk with Jesus. What a great blessing to know I never alone when I walk.

Galatians 2:20 is the foundation of my new re-created life. "I am crucified with Christ: nevertheless 1 live; yet not I, but Christ lives in me: and the life I now live in the flesh I live by the faith of the Son of God, who loved me, and gave himself for me." God put His new life in me in the person of

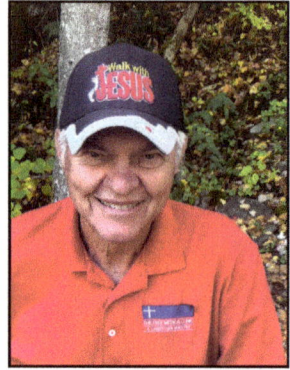

Ray Brown

His Son to replace the old life I had been trying improve. I now realize that truly I am a container for the greatest treasure the world has ever known. Now I can love God as He desires, and with His love working through me I am able to be a beacon of light to a needy world. May you be blessed as the Lord speaks His truths while reading this book.

To the Father be all honor and Glory.

Recalling the Garden

In late spring I took this picture in Cades Cove and the sight caused my pattern of thoughts to focus on the Garden of Eden. I'm not sure why this may have happened unless the shear beauty of the setting or the appearance of the two trees captured my attention. I know it would be impossible to paint a portrait in words which would adequately describe the Garden of Eden, but I will share a few of my thoughts.

I visualize a lush garden of beautiful plants, flowers, trees, with streams of water flowing endlessly bringing necessary ingredients for life to exist. The garden was created to provide food and shelter for the inhabitants who dwelled there. The garden also provided provisions for the animals of the land, the fowl of the air, and aquatic creations present in the streams.

The most significant part of the Garden was God, His presence in the midst of His creation. He was present because He had a strong desire to foster a love relationship with the man and woman He had created to dwell there. His desire was that man would return His love for them based on their own free will. As I recall the events, I remember that man rejected God's instructions and ate the fruit of the forbidden tree, the tree of the knowledge of good and evil. This brought the end of such a magnificent garden and man was expelled to live a life of imperfection in a vastly different setting. This life would last until God sent His Son to earth to initiate the restoration of man to the garden.

What is the application to this story. The two trees are a reminder that man is still faced with a choice. He can eat from the tree of knowledge of good and evil promoted by Satan leading to death, or from the tree of life by believing in our Lord Jesus which leads to life. By believing he is able to receive His eternal life and rejoice in the fact he is always present with the Lord residing as a citizen of heaven.

The Lord began creation for man with a garden and He will end it with a city. The streets will be paved with gold much as the landscape is covered to produce a golden color in the picture. There will only be the tree of life in that city as our Father accomplishes all that He sought from man, an eternal relationship with Father, sons, and daughters sharing love for eternity. Thank you Father for choosing me as one of your sons.

My Christmas Noel

As the season of Christmas nears at our home, I hear the melody of a familiar tune echoing throughout house. The scurrying of busy footsteps racing from room to room placing decorations with the care of a master. Each wreath is hung with precision to radiate the story of a circle of love for all. Nativity sets are strategically placed to provide a witness of the incarnate birth of our savior, Jesus. The tree is trimmed with ornaments old and new, and glistens with pride while beautifully wrapped gifts pose at its feet.

The house has an aroma of Christmas cookies, cakes, and candy being prepared to nourish our family and friends. The rattle of pots and pans is a constant noise filling the air. The sound of dishes being washed is a reminder of the labor being expended.

The lights are all strung to illuminate the beauty that gracefully adorns each nook and cranny. The elves are joyfully playing for all to see. The Santa statues are readied to bring Christmas cheer. The carolers are joyfully humming the tunes of the season. Even the eagle stands eloquently as a wreath is worn to celebrate the season. Candles galore are ready to bring about a flicker of dancing lights. All the work is now finished and my Christmas Noel begins to sing.

You see my Christmas Noel is really a song about my wife, Ethel, who loves Christmas almost as much as life. With a smile on her lips, a twinkle in her eyes, and joy in her heart, her song is being sung for all to be blessed. As family and guests witness her expression of love, they are sure the presence of her Savior is very near. Yes, Christmas has arrived again, and My Christmas Noel, Ethel, is the gift I love more than any I will receive. I treasure the season and embrace the moments for I know my Christmas Noel will be sung again. Thank you Father for again giving the gift of such a beautiful song.

Joy in the Mist

As I anticipated what this day would hold for me, I envisioned a day of peaceful serenity while I once again traveled a portion of the Blue Ridge Parkway. My desire was to find a relaxing spot at the base of a beckoning tree overlooking the beautiful vistas expanding to the far horizons expressing the handiwork of our Lord. I was desiring for Him to paint a picture in my mind that I could transfer to paper which would illustrate the beauty I beheld, as an expression of my gratitude to Him for allowing me to experience another mountaintop day.

The environment in which I was traveling offered a surprise unexpected and unwanted by me as I was driving. While searching for the right spot to satisfy my longings, I was suddenly surrounded by a cloud. The cloud allowed me only a dim view of the sights I dreamed of enjoying. I was gripped with disappointment as my expectations were shattered by another phenomenon of nature. As I proceeded without the best attitude, I discovered a greater lesson while surrounded by the hazy mist.

I experienced the cloud engulfing the forest around me. The content of the cloud consisted of a mist that gently provided moisture to all the vegetation it touched. I saw leaves dancing in the cool breeze as if they were giving thanks for the much-needed drops of water. I observed flowering trees and wild flowers radiating brilliant colors, though encapsulated by a canopy of refreshing mist. I approached a wild turkey rummaging for food, and my presence did not seem to disturb her. I was disappointed in my plans for the day at this moment, but all nature was expressing joy to continue life as orchestrated by our Creator.

Then, as if a veil had been lifted from my presence, the sun burst forth, shining in a backdrop of an endless blue sky elegantly adorned with an array of billowy white clouds. The beauty-laced heavens produced shadows upon the vistas below, as the sun darted in and out of the cloud formations. I have seldom witnessed such beauty. The breathtaking views shown to me were not what I had planned, but it was enough to remind me of the pleasure my Heavenly Father receives as He magnifies His artistic creation for all to see.

So what did I learn today? I learned again that some things that stir my curiosity will only be viewed dimly until the veil is completely lifted. I realize there will be times when I need the refreshing moisture of God's word surrounding me in my periods of dryness. I need for my life to radiate His Son even when viewed dimly by a dark world. I see His presence in a misty cloud about me, and His desire is to have communion with me. So as the vistas came into view briefly, my disappointment was turned to joy as I realized the lesson of the day was better than the one I had planned. I realized again that my Father has provided me a path to follow, a Holy Spirit to be my guide, a Son who died for me, and a communion with Him that is everlasting. May He be greatly praised.

Jesus Found in Unusual Places

Recently, as I walked along a familiar trail I was drawn to this cluster of wildflowers. In my intrigue and imagination I was thinking I must have something to learn from this grouping as I tarried a moment there. The larger flower noticed my lingering and invited me to join the discussion they were having. I inquired about the nature of their discussion, to which he replied, "We are talking to one another as to who we are." I accepted the invitation by relating that the subject was one of my favorites to discuss.

He began to introduce the others in the group to me. He said the young one to his right was a new convert. The one over his left shoulder had just received the revelation of the Spirit of Jesus living in him. The other two older ones and himself were explaining to the group how they had tried to live their lives by doing all the good things they could, but could not find satisfaction in life. He went on to elaborate that self righteousness and futility were the results. They continued that the Holy Spirit revealed to them that Jesus was their life, and this revelation produced a freedom and rest that was impossible to describe.

He then turned his attention back to me and expressed amazement that I was still present and listening attentively. I spoke to them of my agreement with them and thanked them for their faithfulness to share. As I departed, my heart was filled with joy and awe. The lesson I received from this encounter was when I am looking for Jesus, I will find Him even in the most unusual places and circumstances. After all, Jesus is my all in all. Yes, He is the creator of all things and is in all things. Amen.

Friends

In recalling and considering the details along my journey of life, I experience anew the emotions that have stretched me and molded me into who I am. Each season of life seems to bring to the surface circumstances that have either hindered my journey or have brought excitement and encouragement to strengthen my resolve to continue. I have known a life filled with the unexpected, and have walked through the unknown almost daily. Yes, I have lived, not as one who has been given the foreknowledge of what lay ahead, but as one who was given the directions to walk through the circumstances regardless of the pain or joy encountered. How was I enabled to travel such a pathway? How have I overcome the threats of death and despair? How have I celebrated the mountaintop elation of joy? How have I responded to love that seemed to flow by my side like a calming stream? Have I maintained a gentle and contrite spirit as I tried to scale the craggy cliffs of success? Many questions enter my mind as I consider the path of life that was planned for me. One thing I have concluded, I could not have made it alone. The Creator of myself and my journey provided me with an important ingredient to satisfy the helplessness that I often encountered. He provided me with many friends.

Many books have been written to define what makes a person a true friend. I believe there are no words adequate to describe the relational benefits of true friendship. I realize the words I pen will not touch the worth of what a friend means in comforting the needs of others, but I will try to express the necessity of a friend's presence.

As I have walked through the valleys of despair, loneliness, and grief, my vision of the valley was dimmed by the complexity of the situation at hand. Somehow I would block out the beauty and blessings of the valley. I would visualize only the dark clouds of helplessness that seemed to control my every thought. I would miss the real beauty of the valley with its large expanse of meadows awakened daily and glistening with the refreshing dew of morning. Also absent from my view were the flowers opening up, swaying to the tune of a gentle breeze, and the dancing streams that crisscrossed the terrain bringing refreshment to all it touched. So why are valleys referred to in our lives as disappointment instead of joy? It appears my view of the valley had been distorted by my focus on the problem at hand, which would allow darkness to prevail. In silence I would deal with the disappointment as if it was the tragedy of all tragedies. During the periods of doubt, the clouds of darkness would fill the sky and any ray of light producing relief was unable to filter through. The product of these thoughts would produce such enemies as self pity, loneliness, and self control. In every valley I have experienced the beauty of realizing that I really was not alone. The Creator has been faithful in sending friends to walk with me out of the darkness. I could once again view the valley's beauty for nature's intended purpose, that is, the learning garden that helps to produce who I really am, an example of Jesus. He uses a tool to show me He really cares for me, a friend. A friend is someone who cares and really means it.

I have walked on mountaintops of happiness that I hoped would never end, as the vistas seen from the highest peaks would bring awe and excitement to me. Their presence has never grown old. Their beauty is enhanced by the flowering springtime, the coolness found in the summer, the hues of fall colors, and a blanket of snow producing a mystifying beauty of winter. The excitement of the mountaintop is wonderful but it would be a selfish extension of my old nature if I did not want to share the joy and encouragement received on the pinnacle of the mountain. Once again a friend has always been provided to listen to my story, and rejoice with me while I related the good news allowed by our Heavenly Father. A friend is someone who finds joy in my presence and really means it.

Streams of water have always somehow spoken to me. I love to settle near a stream to meditate and glean a message that only a stream can impart. A stream can relate a beneficial story when time is taken to observe its flow as it peacefully supplies the needs for all of mankind. I enjoy a calm stream which seems to exude love to me. The streams that are mentioned in Psalms 46 illustrate such love. "There is a river whose streams make glad the city of God." The Lord has sent friends to walk beside me through the years of my journey. These are the ones who love me in a greater sense, and would be willing to die for me. He provided such a friend in my wife, Ethel, who daily is the calm stream that flows by my side and expresses unconditional love for me. Yes, a friend is someone who says, "I love you" and really means it.

As my journey continued, I found myself entering the arena of what man referred to as success in life. I often found myself grasping for the next step that would lead me to the top of the craggy cliffs of success. In reality, I ventured to think the next level of satisfaction would be the achievement of success as defined by man. Struggling for monetary gain and a sense of accomplishment, I steadily pulled myself upward, though my inner being knew the real source of success was a blessing from the Lord, rather than a reward of my own efforts. I often spoke of my doing, while neglecting the testimony of my Savior as the provider. Enter again the presence of friends to correct my misguided quest. A friend who may not have been as successful, but would express love to me in a way that would show me success was not what I had attained, but rather who I really was. Many friends failed to ascend to the crest of monetary gain but neither murmured or complained. I was befriended by people who helped me recognize who I was in Christ and the joy derived in sharing my God-made success with others. A true friend is someone who says "I understand" and really means it.

I have tried to express a few of my thoughts about being and having a friend. May this brief presentation plant a seed in your being about the necessity of having and being a friend. The Lord has been so gracious to provide me help along the journey with friends whom I cherish very much. The ultimate friend is the Lord Jesus who gave His life for me and promised never to leave me or forsake me. He desires that I live in His house forever and by His grace I wish to fulfill His desire. In closing I would like to say to all who read this essay, thank you for being my friend because I know you really mean it. In response, I would like to reply that I am your friend and I really mean it.

Fountain of Living Water

In describing the fountain I noticed a pipe extending above the surface of the water. A pump which drew water from the pond forced the water through the exposed pipe producing a beautiful phenomenon for all to see. The pipe seemed to be at rest and joyful as the water passed through its innermost being. I tried to imagine how many people would be touched as they viewed the pipe without the water flow? Would the pipe try to produce a flow of water on his own effort? Did the pipe really know who he was? A few questions that I pondered.

Spiritually, I envisioned myself as the pipe.

I see Jesus' presence within me as the pump. I see His life flowing through me as the living water. As the water flows out of my being peace, joy, and love radiates to a world in need of hope. His life in me is everlasting and will flow forever. I have entered His rest and depend on Him to accomplish His purpose in me. Yes, there is a fountain that flows through me which continues to cleanse me of my sins with the blood He shed on Calvary. It is so wonderful to know that I am a vessel of clay who contains a precious treasure in the person of Jesus, the Son of God. May I be faithful to allow Him to live His life through me. I have written this in the first person, but I want you to know that I see Jesus in each of you and in I rejoice that we are one in Him.

Come Thou
And Walk With Me

Come thou and walk with me " were the first words I heard on my music app as I opened the front door to begin my morning walk. My excited response was one of great expectations, and my steps quickened as I bounded down our front steps. After a brief conversation with a neighbor, we continued on our way only to hear "Turn Your Eyes Upon Jesus" as I reinserted my earbuds. I received the message that Jesus wanted the two of us to walk together, and today He wanted my full attention. As we continued walking, I noticed the mountains were hazy and their beauty was hidden, revealing to me that from an earthly view our future looks uncertain at the present time. I lifted my eyes to see a clear blue sky proclaiming His grace and glory unfettered by a wispy cloud or streaking jet stream trail, reminding me that from a heavenly view our future is certain and our destination has been completed and paid for by Him,

Our walk continued with a brotherly conversation. We spent a little time in silence and solitude as we walked through a small cemetery reminiscing days past when times were different. As we exited the cemetery another musical refrain touched my heart. The words I heard were "He walks with me and talks with me and tells me I am His own." I found so much assurance as these words were shared at this moment.

Further down the path my expectations begin to build again as I thought some earth-moving revelation might lie ahead. To my disappointment, my phone went dead. No more musical refrains, yet He seemed to say, "Now just you and I can walk and talk together." And so we did. It was a wonderful day of fellowship with Him. I know He walks every day with me because He resides within me, but it was extra special that He asked me to walk with Him today. When I returned home, I had walked 7.5 miles, strengthened by His joy within me. He is so good and His love is everlasting.

Abiding in Christ

As I review my life in comparison to the words found in John 15, I find a striking number of similarities. The relationship between the vine and the branches are the basis for portraying my relationship with Jesus. I visualize my life in Him as a beautiful painting by His hand that will have everlasting significance. A broken branch placed into the wounded side of a vine for the Father's eternal glory.

When I was a young lad, the Lord opened His arms with a heart of love that I could not resist and said, "Come unto me." Unknown in part at the time, I did not realize I was surrendering my life and my all to Him for eternity. Even so, I went to Him realizing I could not see Him. I believed Him which could only have happened by the faith received from Him. Little did I know that at the moment I believed, He placed me in His Son and I became one spirit with Him. (1 Cor. 6:17)

As the parable in John 15 reveals, I became a new twig grafted into the vine of eternal life. He then said, "Abide in Me." Now began a new venture of life as a branch positioned in an eternal vine. Prior to this time I was dwelling as a branch in a vine amid surroundings of my natural physical birth. A vine dresser came near me one day saying, "If you will come with me and allow me to place you in my vine, I will permit you to live forever and bear fruit so beautiful that other branches will also desire to be a part of my vine." I looked around my environment and saw deeds of evil, chaos, and despair all leading to death. Without hesitation I said yes to His invitation, placing my trust and dependence upon Him. I was concerned about my past life and I related to Him that I needed to clean myself up.

He immediately began washing me and voicing words of grace, caring, and hope to me. When He finished I seemed to feel strangely clean inside and out. He gently caressed me in His loving hands and took me to His vineyard which had been growing forever. He, with great precision, opened a wound in the side of His vine and placed me into His presence. I will never forget the sap of the vine that ran down my young body, as I imagined the pain suffered for me to become a part of Him. As the vine dresser turned as if to walk away, He touched me and love surrounded Him as He spoke the following words to me, "There will be an unseen person that will come and seal the union that has been made between you and the Vine.

"Really you have nothing to fear because He is actually My Spirit," He told me. "After His work is finished you will be a part of the Vine that has always been and forever will be. He will stay with you and teach you about the Vine and your relationship to the Vine. And everything He tells you will be truth." After I could hear Him no longer, my mind began to wander. If I cannot see this person, l wondered if he's a ghost. I feel so wonderful around the Vine Dresser and I am so happy He has chosen me. I really trust Him and believe everything He says. Wow, I wonder if the one He's sending to seal my union is the Holy Ghost? I'm sure in time I will know. I am so happy, this is just too good to be true, but I know it is. I am in a vine that is eternal and actually has become my life, and cared for by a vine dresser who has always been. I think the next time I talk to Him I will call Him Father.

As I grew in knowledge and stature, I began to notice the beautiful fruit weighing down the other branches of which I was a part. I was awestruck by such beauty that was impossible to describe. I was disappointedly affected inwardly when a voice inside me said, "not yet." My maturing process in the vine required much tending and care by the keeper of the vine. Many times pruning was necessary, and wow did that hurt. Again I heard the inner voice say it is good for you, and you will be aware that I am still with you. Cleansing had to be performed from time to time to rid my foliage of the stains of life that prevented the light from penetrating my being. The light was necessary to enhance my growth in the maturing process. Later in the nurturing process, a yearning developed within me to bear fruit. I thought how much longer? Are we there yet? I so desire to bear this beautiful expression of who I am designed to be. The Keeper of the Vine kept tending and I kept waiting. Oh how hard it is to wait when you get a glimpse of the future. Patience seemed to be my hardest task yet. I thought surely by this time I could bear fruit, but I received a startling message from the vine stating that I could do nothing within myself. You must depend on me to do anything. This was something that I really had not given much thought. It seemed logical to me that where the fruit hung was where it was produced. Now I began to realize that this wasn't about me, but about the Vine, though I did sense He needed me to be a part. He was definitely excited to be able to use me. He then related to me that He was providing nourishment to strengthen me, so

I would be able to bear the fruit He produced through me. Wow, what a revelation; I thought I had to do it. It would be a privilege if I could do it. He said, "You will be seen, but I want to receive the credit for bearing the fruit. It is because you were placed in Me and I nourished and kept you until now that you have become strong enough to bear the fruit I produce in you. I am well pleased with you; remember my nutrients will sustain you. I am always with you moment by moment bringing forth life in you. You have to depend on Me and recognize Me as the source of your existence."

Shortly thereafter one beautiful spring day, I awoke from my night of rest to discover something new occurring near my beautiful clean foliage. A bud was formed. Was this the beginning of the fruit bearing process? The Vine told me, "yes, you have become strong enough to bear fruit and to withstand the storms of life." I never again questioned my position, my function, or my dependence upon the vine. I noticed some branches developed quickly and others slowly, but many characteristics were common to all. We bore beautiful alluring fruit, we were all a part of the vine, we shared a common love for each other, and a joy that sung love songs heard in the heavenly realms. What a beautiful gift was given to me as I was taken from my past darkness to become a shining light to the world bearing fruits of hope.

As I personified the vine and the branch parable, He has taught me that I am His son, that He has placed me in Jesus. Jesus is my life as revealed and sustained by the Holy Spirit that is being expressed through my earthly body. The fruit I bear is produced by the vine of which I am joined, enabling my Father to be glorified as more sons and daughters are drawn to Him. He has chosen me and made me one with Jesus and Himself by the power of the Holy Spirit, and also one with you who have also been chosen. I choose to abide with Him in answer to His plea. To know Him better, to continue experiencing His love and basking in His joy, is the desire of my heart. I depend on my Father to keep me abiding in Him, because I know it is not possible in my strength. Thank you, Jesus, for securing my eternal communion with You.

Thank you for using me to bear the fruit of your righteousness, the fruit of the Holy Spirit consisting of love, joy, peace, patience, kindness, goodness, faithfulness, gentleness, and self-control, and also the fruit of my lips that acknowledges your name with a sacrifice of praise.

Does This Lonely Flower Have a Purpose?

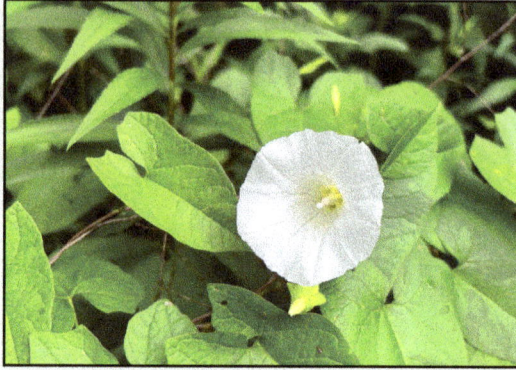

For a few days I have been observing this lone flower. Why was I so drawn to this ordinary looking wildflower? Was it because it was isolated and surrounded by other vegetation? Was it because it struggled through a recent storm and rising flood waters that it survived for a purpose? What was the source of its strength? Why do I think like this? What is in me that would make me want to spend any time viewing what I perceive to be a lonely flower? My answer came as I recalled Eph. 1:10, "That in the dispensation of the fullness of times he might gather together in one all things in Christ, both which are in heaven, and which are on earth, even in Him." Also Col. 1:16,17: "For by Him were all things created, that are in heaven, and that are in earth, visible and invisible, whether they be thrones, or dominions, or principalities, or powers—all things were created by Him, and for Him; and he is before all things, and by Him all things consist." And Col. 3:11 contains the phrase: "but Christ is all and in all." This occasion illustrated and confirmed to me the revelation that Christ is my only life. Christ is in all things, even this lonely flower is not alone, but has the presence of Christ abiding within to proclaim the glory of God to a needy world. Do we see Christ in all things? Most of all do we see Christ in ourselves? He has been present from the first time we believed. What a wonderful plan our Father created for our salvation. Now we are able to enter His rest.

Thoughts of the Day

T he trumpets are posed to sound forth God's glory at His command. The saints on earth clothed in the white raiment of His righteousness gaze expectantly toward heaven awaiting His appearing. Will it be today? Maybe or maybe not.

As I give thought to what I've seen and heard today, how do I then live? I was reminded of a song that states, "Each day is like heaven my heart overflows." This is the way I desire to live. As I live each day, I realize that each day is like heaven, because out of me flows a river of His grace as His Son's life is being formed in me. So is His appearing today? Maybe, but if not, each day is like heaven until He says, today is the day.

The Lord's Voice Upon the Waters

When I took this picture I was reminded of the scripture found in Psalms 29:3—the voice of the Lord is upon the waters. I pondered, does He want to speak to me from this beautiful scene? Does He just want me to describe what I see? I was puzzled that words did not come to mind from viewing such a beautiful scene. After much thought the following words depict what I saw and heard. He will lead me beside still water and restore my soul. The scene is very restful, be still my soul and wait for Him. I notice the water is still with reflections upon its surface, inspiring the thoughts of living water. I also see the reflections of the trees as how I am being transformed into His image for His glory. The water looks peaceful and illustrates a peace that surpasses all understanding, which is helpful to me as I cope with these turbulent times. Yes, I do have peace like a river that continually floods my soul. Our Father, in His great love for us has planted us like trees beside the still waters. We shall not fear because of the confidence we have in Him, created by our trust in Him. We will bear the fruit He produces in us, and reap the joy and gratitude in our souls for the privilege of knowing Him. He is still God and is very much in control as He continues to build His body, which goes forward with love to touch our world. Yes there is a river that flows by the throne of God and He is in the midst of Her. Psalms 46:4-5.

Blooms in the Bog

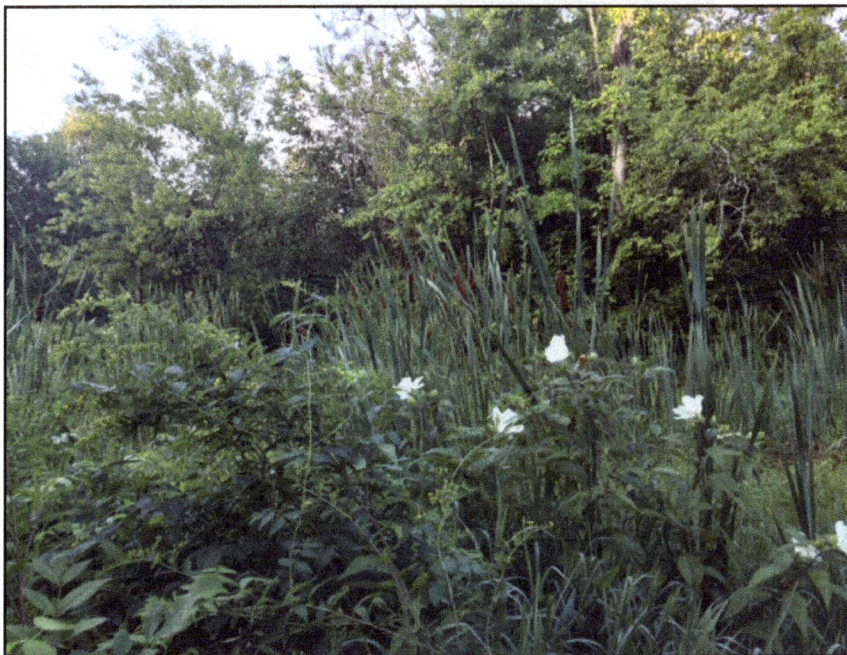

G od has created such a beautiful world according to His ultimate plan. What man could have envisioned planting these beautiful plants in such a swampy area? These plants will be viewed by only a few yet they are displaying the outward beauty that was contained in the seed from which they began. I noticed that no two blooms were exactly alike, yet they were displaying the glory of God, fulfilling their purpose for being.

As my thoughts turned to man, I could see a comparison with these plants. We have been planted in a swampy world. Each of us are different in so many ways, yet we transmit the beauty of the life of Christ to the world, a beauty that is mostly ignored by the masses.

Though we are different in appearance, we who are born again contain the same seed, Jesus. As we allow His life to flow through us, we show forth the glory of God which is our ultimate purpose of being. Yes, Christ in us is the hope of glory, not only for us, but for a needy world. Col. 1:27

The Love of God

I returned today to my walking routine after being hindered by illness. As I was walking, the song "The Love of God" by Guy Pernod played through my earbuds. The Holy Spirit directed my thoughts to the cross, which I deem to be God's greatest outpouring of love to me. The ultimate sacrifice was made for me. I have often wondered, "why me?" The only answer to me is that I am not able to grasp the vastness of God's love. He loves me so much that if I had been the only one in need of His sacrifice, He would have gone to the cross for me. All of this display of love for me is a part of his ultimate intention and plan for mankind.

Now I began thinking of Galatians 2:20. I am crucified with Christ. Was I on the cross with Christ? Nevertheless I live: yet not I but Christ liveth in me. Does Christ really live in me? And the life I NOW live in the flesh, I live by the faith of the Son of God, who loved me and gave Himself for me. Is the new life He gave me really His life? Do I really live by His faith instead of mine? My answer to these questions is YES. The scriptures relate to me that Jesus is the Life, truth, love, peace, joy, goodness, and faith to name a few attributes of His character. What makes all of this work? My love affair with Him. The question I am confronted with is the same question presented to Peter in John 21:15: "Ray, lovest thou me?" My reply is, "yes, Lord, I do love you."

Ray Brown

Life Filled with Circumstances

Walking this morning I was faced with a familiar dilemma. I faced the darkness of a foot bridge that was shrouded with summer growth. This bridge spans a swampy area of a larger pond. Snakes have been known to spend time on the bridge, as well as menacing insects populating the area. As these thoughts went through my mind, I noticed sufficient light filtering through the overgrown vegetation to allow me to pass safely over the bridge. After safely passing through darkened area, I was met with brilliant light to brighten my path as I pursued the purpose ahead of me for the day.

So what have I learned today? That no matter what situation I face, I will have sufficient light to see me through whatever lies ahead. Jesus is the light. He is really the light I see in my circumstances. Because He lives in us, we are the light of the world shining forth through every circumstance. His light is everlasting as depicted by the light on my path as I emerged from the darkness engulfing the bridge. Each situation I confront will teach me who I really am and better prepare me as His son, to enter His house. "I Surrender All" was playing as I crossed the bridge. I have to surrender my old life and accept His to realize all He has planned for me. May our walks on His paths bring glory to Him.

Our Journey on Our Path of Life

In recent days I have been reminded of the truth found in Psalms 16:11. The initial part of that verse relates to each of us that our Father makes known our path of life.

I love to hike familiar paths in the fall of the year. I have pictured a couple of trails that I'm sharing with you.

As I traveled on the trails I noticed that fallen leaves had a change in nature. They had fallen from lofty heights, admired by many, to now lie on the ground, crumbling, and scattered by the footsteps of hikers, as they struggled to stay on the path to reach their destinations. There have been many times when I was unsure if I was still on a path, because the path was obscured or poorly marked. I can remember the joy I felt when I realized I was on the right path and my safety secured. Many lessons can be learned as we concentrate on our divinely-orchestrated path.

As I was walking on my usual trail the other day, I noticed the leaf-covered trail was reminding me of our present day chaos and confusion. I began asking our Father for answers to the many questions I have.

I looked down as the trail ahead cleared and I saw the answer. A leaf in the perfect shape of a heart caught my attention. It's as if the Lord whispered it will be when man's heart is changed by belief in Me that he will be able to experience My love for him, which will enable him to walk in love. As far as the path of life, I realized I was on His path made for me because He revealed His love in this most unusual way to me. I rejoiced and praised Him again for the revelation of His love for me in this spontaneous moment as I searched for answers. The path of life has many challenges for us as we continue to grow in Him. May we experience His love and joy as we walk on the path He has revealed to us. He desires for us to love Him regardless of the circumstances we encounter on the path.

Now I See

A few weeks ago while I was struggling with blurry vision resulting from shingles in my eye, a friend of mine shared the account of the blind man in Mark 8:22-25: "And He (Jesus) cometh to Bethsaida; and they bring a blind man unto Him. And He took the blind man by the hand, and led him out of the town; and when He had spit on his eyes, and put His hands upon him, He asked him if he saw anything. And he looked up, and said, I see men like trees walking. After He put His hands again upon his eyes, and made him look up; and he was restored, and saw every man clearly." These verses ministered to me as I was dealing with not seeing clearly. After meditating on these verses I began to see another meaning for me to receive. I began to think about the gap created between the first touch of Jesus and the second touch to the man's eye. What I saw was a gap in time when I was saved as a child by God's grace, and the spiritual revelation of being in Christ made real to me about 7 years ago. Now I see this gap in time was used to prepare me for the life He has in store for me when He calls me to live in His house. I was reminded that as a child I spoke as a child, but when I became a man I put away childless things. In other words now I can see with spiritual understanding more clearly as my Father reveals His purpose and His plans for my life. He has placed His son in me to live His life in me and to be my all in all. Though my understanding will continue to become clearer throughout eternity, I feel so blessed to receive from Him. I have a most wonderful Father and I am so happy to be His son.

Leaves of Love

A s I was walking this morning, I felt so surrounded by our Father's love. My feet shuffled through a carpet of many fallen leaves that covered my swampy path. Leaves were falling around me to paint a premature picture of the fall season approaching.

Suddenly I became aware that many of the leaves were heart shaped, and began to remind me of heart-felt experiences of my past. I noticed some of the leaves brought to my remembrance times of joy, triumph, failure, sadness, kindness, grief, doubt, love, fellowship, and aloneness; just to name a few. To me these are only expressions of my heart as a part of my education in the schoolhouse of life. All of which are working for my good.

I tried to form a heart with the heart-shaped leaves that spoke to me. I noticed the heart I created was far from a perfect heart, but the invisible heart you see surrounding my imperfect creation is the perfect heart of God pouring out His love upon me and making me pure. What a wonderful Father we have Who welcomes us into His lap as His dear child. Thank you, Father for once again showing me your love in this most unusual way. Yes the leaves fulfill their purpose in allowing the love of God to be expressed through them to a needy soul. May I do the same as I allow Him to express His love through me to everyone in need.

I'll Meet You In The Morning

As I began my daily venture of walking a familiar path, the thoughts of an old gospel hymn came to mind, "I'll Meet You in the Morning." I am always excited when early promptings produce an expectancy in me that may be a word of enlightenment from the Lord. I naturally began thinking of how He would meet me when all around me the deadness of nature was present, as the darkness of late winter prevails and the fullness of spring is still in the birthing stage.

I journeyed through a swampy area of the path, and paused on a little bridge to view a sight I had seen many times previously. I was drawn to the picture of nature I was witnessing, and stood peering longer than usual at the scene before me. I saw an old tree that had fallen across the stream that meandered though the swampy land. I saw other trees, large and small, lining the banks of the creek near the fallen one, as their mirror image was reflecting on the surface of the stream. I looked above to view the beautiful blue sky, which added color to the picture being formed as the sun highlighted the landscape. What a beautiful picture to behold. So what am I looking at today? What is the story in this picture?

I see an old tree that has finished his purpose on earth. I see a tree that was born by the Creator to live out his purpose in an area considered undesirable to most, and his life was not to be noticed by many. The seed from which he began contained all that was necessary for him to live, grow, and exist in his surroundings. He grew tall and was blessed with great strength as He endured the storms of life. He received nourishment from the stream of life that flowed near and through him. As a result, he was able to produce fruit in abundance for the world to see. He had provided a home for the fowls of the air. He was a shelter for animals as fear and storms threatened their existence. He was well-respected by all who new him.

Now the time for him to depart the life he had known was present. His heart had ceased to beat, his limbs bore fruit on longer, his strength had departed, and he now laid lifeless in the stream that had been the main source of his life. I see other trees bent forward as if mourning his death. I see smaller trees as the result of the fruit he produced. I notice their limbs are uplifted, as if praising and thanking the Creator for the life the deceased had lived before them. I see other friends and family lining the surroundings, paying tribute to a lifelong friend.

As I have personified the life and death of an old tree, I was able to see many spiritual applications. I will only enumerate a few. I see new birth as a result of the seed (Jesus) that the Father has placed in us. I see a river of living water flowing through us to produce life and to give love to a world in need. I see fruit being naturally produced by the life within us. I see some who live their lives without being noticed by the multitudes. I see all believers as instruments of God, spreading His message by the lives they live. I see the least of us bringing pleasure to our Father. I believe the Lord met me this morning to once again relate His story to me through my natural surroundings. May the life and death of this old tree be an encouragement to us as we daily encounter the darkness produced in this world.

What Lies Around the Bend

Walking this morning I stopped on these railroad tracks and begin to ponder the thoughts of what might lie ahead around the bend of the tracks. Would it be a gloomy encounter of the unknown as portrayed by the constant newscasts that fill the airwaves or would a joyful experience lie ahead? As I continued on my path, I came upon a sight that lifted my soul out of despondency. A dogwood tree rising above its entangled surroundings reminded me of the greatest blessings of life. The tree was signifying to me all that Jesus overcame in our world as a man, and at the same time, was proclaiming: I lived, I died, I arose again to live that you might have life, and I promise never to leave you alone no matter what is around the bend. What a beautiful answer to my pondering. May you rest assured today that He is ever present with us.

Mystique of a Waterfall

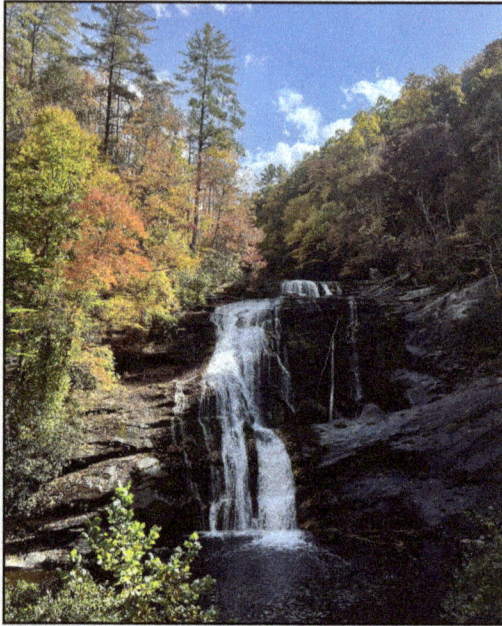

Recently as I photographed a small waterfall, my mind seemed to be fixed on the beauty that only a waterfall could project. My thoughts raced in various directions as I considered nature's display of such beauty. I asked why I travel many miles to marvel at the magnificence of a plunging stream? Why do I hike up rugged steep mountainous terrain to be entertained by a waterfall? Why do I never tire of seeing even the smallest of waterfalls? How does a waterfall personify my personal journey and my God-given purpose as I walk daily through life's challenges? Many, many questions arrive when I begin to ponder these awe-striking phenomena.

As a mountainous stream is formed and begins its journey to the valleys below, I wonder what each droplet is thinking as they begin their travel to their prescribed destination. They seem to realize the purpose within as they fearlessly begin their flow. They seem to be encouraged by the fact that others will benefit from their purpose. They seem unfettered by the dangers that are apparent as the unknown lurks ahead. An excitement is present as they ponder the witness they will display to others.

As the droplets travel in unison forming a sparkling stream, they flow over rocks, and sediments of vegetation that lines their route. They travel onward in peaceful serenity until in the distance a deafening roar is heard. The unknown is about to become known, but what is this interruption to their peaceful surroundings? Little did they realize that they were about to be a spectacle of grandeur to be viewed by many witnesses.

While their speed draws them closer to the thunderous noise ahead each droplet is gripped with fear. Trembling is evident and a desire to seek safety, as thoughts of the comfort of a gentle stream permeates their minds is present. Finally they arrive at the eerie moment of destiny and without hesitation they exhibit their trust they possess in their Creator as they begin their descent to the waters below. All of a sudden they are floating through the air, forming a beauty that mystifies mankind. As they descend, the sun penetrates their very being producing a beautiful rainbow arching over the backdrop of falling water. They are objects of photos, movies, and eyes of amazement as they plunge into the stream below to continue their journey. Each droplet is a part of a fascination that has drawn many visitors to be affected by their life's journey.

They travel forward and become aware of the surroundings that enhance the purpose of their mission. They see trees offering thanksgiving for their presence. They see various shades of moss forming a velvet pallet on rocks along the way. Flowers line their banks and appear to sway continuously in a seemingly endless breeze. Wild creatures are viewed quenching their thirst as many droplets surrender their all to satisfy the destiny to which they were called. Yes, finally the importance of being a part of the mystique of a waterfall is being realized.

The waterfall is personified to teach us about our life's journey. We see that the Lord has designed in us a purpose to recognize. At times it will cause us to fear and to seek safety erroneously in our old lives. To some of us it may cost the ultimate sacrifice of our life to provide an eternal redemption for those around us. Sometimes we may question our existence and be unaware of the beauty of the purpose given. On a positive note, the waterfall teaches you a greater level of trust. It teaches that we are reflecting God's glory to many witnesses. It relates to us that we are completely dependent on our heavenly Father for our provision and protection. It enforces the fact that we are a part of God's redemptive plan, and that the mystery performed in our lives by our union with Jesus will draw men to Him.

Thank you, Lord Jesus, for the beauty of a waterfall that reminds me of the beauty of your salvation. For the picture portrayed in a waterfall that expresses your desire that your eternal purpose be made known. That purpose being to know Jesus so that your house will be filled with many sons and daughters.

Seaside Sunrise

A sunrise by the seaside is always an awe-inspiring event. As the dawning of a new day emerges from the darkness of night, light in its brilliance chases the darkness to the far horizon. Many events begin to happen that would suggest this to be a perfectly organized spectacle. How can a description of the beauty and astonishment be penned by a viewer who realizes the scene will be repeated in 24 hours?

The distant horizon paints a picture on a canvas embedded in the minds of men. The viewer witnesses a band of dark coloration touching the distant expanse of sea.

Orange hues are positioned atop the dark band as if forcing it into the depths of the sea. Above the hues of orange, the sky is illuminated with a beautiful golden glow. Not a single cloud is sighted to magnify the beauty that is present. Amazing wonder abounds, as the sun sheds its beams upon the earth and sea. The colors of dawn abate and yield to a blue sky that signals a new day has begun.

As sunbathers bask in the morning sun, they are entertained by the graceful flight of seagulls, the diving precision of the pelicans, the foot speed of the sandpipers, and the shyness of the sand crabs.

Regally designed butterflies are visible, soaring to heights deemed possible only by eagles. The branches of palm trees lay silent, waiting for the morning breeze to lift them in praise for a new day. The sea is calm as its serenity signals a peaceful day of rest is at hand.

Walkers are plentiful, trekking the shoreline and beginning another day of their life's journey. Their thoughts vary as they enjoy the splendor of the landscape surrounding them. Some are happy to escape the riggers of everyday routine. Some are enjoying the first days of life together.

Troubles due to circumstances and situations of life cloud the minds of the weary. Others are rejoicing over success in the workplace with elated faces. Some are marveling how God could create such beauty, and allow them the privilege to visit.

The events present in the dawning of a new day reminds me of my dependence on my Heavenly Father to provide the necessities for life to exist. Each creature is dependent upon Him to sustain life. He has created all things for His pleasure and is willing to share His goodness with all who will receive. The sea with its expanse and depth reminds me of the many mysteries of God. Some He wishes to share, while others we can only imagine in this life.

As the waves ebb and flow a strange silence surrounds me as the presence of God is apparent. He is revealing to me the necessity to wait on Him in silence as he unveils His plan for me today. He desires for me to be willing to receive what He wants to give, so I wait. A beautiful morning by the sea has begun. The colors are magnificent, the grandeur unmatched, the mysteries remain intact, and the presentation is indescribable. Only God.

Make Me a Sanctuary

As I was walking this morning, I listened to an old praise chorus entitled "Lord Prepare Me to be a Sanctuary." Then I began thinking about the finished work of Jesus according to the plan of our Father. This chorus should be sung in the past tense. The following is my version of the song: "Lord *you have prepared me* to be a sanctuary, pure and holy, tried and true, and with thanksgiving I *am* a living sanctuary for you."

Yes the Lord prepared us to be a sanctuary for Him. All who believe become His sanctuary, where He chooses to dwell. I am so thankful for our Father's plan to daily form us to be like Him.

A Bottle of Dasani — A Picture of Grace

Recently, while enjoying my daily walk I met my friend Mike. We chatted for a few minutes exchanging our thoughts and spiritual revelations that had impacted our lives. Our conversation ended when I told Mike I needed to continue my walk. Mike immediately offered me a bottle of water to accompany me. I politely refused and told him I would be fine. He continued by saying that he had some cold water he could get for me. Again, I refused his offer and told him when I drink cold water while I'm hot, it upsets my stomach. He continued by telling me he had plenty in the garage at room temperature if I preferred. I declined his offer again and told him I would be fine. As I started to leave, he shared that he would leave a bottle of water on his mailbox and if I needed it on my way, I could take it. I said thanks Mike, but I should be okay.

As I continued on my journey, I began to think about Mike's desire to share a bottle of water with me. I asked myself if I had denied Mike a blessing of giving. Have I refused his offer of love to me? Did he sense a need that I had overlooked? Did I miss Jesus wanting to speak to me through Mike? Questions I pondered as I wondered also about his persistency.

As I approached his home on my return, I noticed on his mailbox stood a bottle of water. My thirst level became more prominent as I gazed at the bottle of water. Out of respect for my friend I took the bottle of water and began to quench my thirst. I sent Mike a text thanking him for the water. He replied, "you are welcome my friend." I realized that this was a Jesus incident because He had also referred to me as his friend in John 15.

Later I began to analyze this incident. The first thought I had was the persistent nature of our Father in offering His grace to mankind. The water I accepted was sufficient to satisfy my thirst. I recalled how God's grace was sufficient to satisfy my longing to have my sins forgiven and to be reconciled with Him in my conversion experience. I could see our Father's expression of love for me through a simple bottle of water offered to me. I witnessed Jesus speaking through my friend, Mike, to meet a need I had overlooked. In my exchange with Mike, I saw the blessing received in loving one another as Christ loves us, and I saw the bottle of water as a reminder of when I thirst there is a fountain of the water of life freely given to me. I am so thankful I accepted the offer of a bottle of water so Jesus could remind me of His endless grace.

That day Jesus taught me how He could use the little things in life to remind me of His eternal truth. Thank you, Jesus, for your presence in me and for a friend willing to share his love with me.

A Glimpse of Unaware Blessings

When this picture was taken, I was completely unaware. My focus, at that moment, was centered on the thousands of Purple Martins returning to this lake island to roost. It is a daily event that draws many spectators to witness the phenomena. A friend snapped the picture while I was enthralled by the happenings surrounding me. When I viewed the photo, I was moved spiritually to record my thoughts.

The photo reveals an enormous amount of truth of which adequate space is not available to record. God's grace is so immense that no boundaries exist to contain what our Father has granted us in His grace. I will list a few expressions of His grace that come to mind as I view this picture. These will be truths that were given to me of which I was unaware at the moment I said, "I believe."

By His divine power He has given me all things that pertain to life and godliness. He has given me great and precious promises that I may be a partaker of His divine nature. He has placed His incorruptible seed in me. He has reconciled me to himself. He has justified me by the blood of His son, Jesus. He has placed His son in me in whom I have wisdom, righteousness, sanctification, and redemption. I have received His eternal light which shines through me. I received the life of Jesus which is eternal.

God became my Father by my rebirth and adoption into His family. He now refers to me as His son and joint heir with Jesus. I truly am a new creation.

As I continue to view the photo, I see a continuous flow of God's love for me as our relationship grows. I see His promise are yes and amen and will always be true because He cannot lie. I have listed only a small portion of what I received as I was birthed into His family. One last thing I would like to note. It appears that God is extending His hand to grasp mine. He reminded me that He knew that I had experienced trials, grief, disappointments, and temptations which have occurred while on my journey in the darkness of this world. He seems to say I just want to comfort you with the knowledge that you haven't been walking through past events alone. As you have been on your journey, I have been holding your hand and I will never leave you or forsake you. How amazing is the grace of my Father? I can only with thanksgiving stand in awe of what He has done.

My Personified Friends

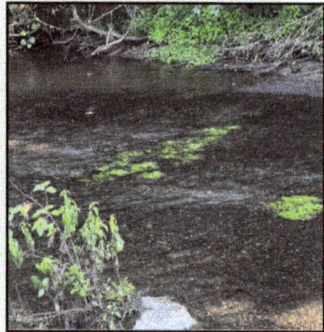

Today I began my daily walk with only a couple of thoughts occupying my mind. One was to complete my annual attempt to walk of ten percent of my age in miles. Another was thanksgiving for my health to even consider a quest of 8.3 miles.

As I continued on my walk, I began to notice familiar sights lining my pathway. I noticed many flowers, berries, trees, streams, and even insects that I had personified in the past, now were my lifelong friends. It is as if they knew the day and time I would attempting this journey. I was so happy to see them as they seemed to be cheering for me, which was such an encouragement to me as I walked. The flowers arrayed in brilliant colors, the trees lowering their branches to offer me high fives, the pokeberries hanging from the vine for a glimpse as I passed. I was overwhelmed as I thought of the stories we had shared with each other, and now their presence was causing another story to come into existence.

I imagined this scene to be a picture of heaven as I walked through the entrance to eternally fellowship with my Father, who by virtue of His great love for me paid the price for me to be present. Along the walk I see many acquaintances who without their knowledge, had a profound influence on my life. Then I can see others shouting thanksgivings toward me for the impact I had on them, often without my knowledge. Some I knew while others seemed to be total strangers to me. My only explanation of this event is that my Father works through me to accomplish His purpose.

So as I have returned home after accomplishing my goal today, I am so thankful for the lessons that have been expressed to me by many of the participants in nature. A few examples come to mind of past experiences. The peace present by the streams as if they were the rivers of living water. The flowers who have represented the glory of God in relating spiritual truths to me. The fluttering butterflies that exemplified joy. The trees and the leaves in the last photo that constantly remind me of the Father's love for me.

I have learned today of my Father's sufficiency as I surrender my life to Him. I am constantly amazed by the goodness and love lavished upon me. Thank you, Father, for including me as part of your wonderful family.

Reminders

few of the reminders I encountered today to emphasize the need to center my thoughts on Him.

Honeysuckle blossoms along a babbling brook offering up joyful praise and a sweet aroma of incense to our Father this morning at the dawning of a new day.

A reminder to me as we begin today in communion with Him we are also a sweet aroma to Him. I experience great joy and offer praise to Him as I realize His light flows out of us like a river of living water bringing hope to all it touches.

A dove walked across my path to remind me of the peace that is available to me as I walk the path of life in these troubled times. May our thoughts be centered on Him today.

Shadows

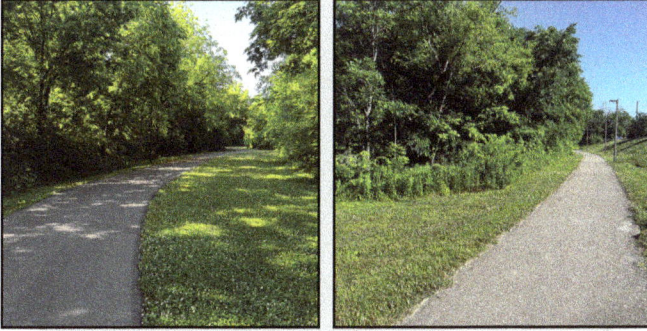

A conscious awareness of a new message came alive today as I began to take notice of shadows that darkened my chosen path. I also noticed light breaking through the shadows detailing the forms of the objects being projected. The images reminded me of a carpet being laid before me as I hiked this familiar trail. My thoughts were concentrated on the sight as I recalled that no shadow could be produced if light wasn't present. A deeper perspective entered my mind as I saw the light being an actual part of the shadows.

The shadows I was viewing today were from different trees that lined a winding creek adding beauty to my walk. The images the trees cast on the ground before me indicated different stages of growth. Some were very tall revealing maturity had been reached, while others were small as life was young within their being, but regardless of age they all cast a shadow that relates a precious story that changed the world. What is that story?

As I continued my hike, I noticed the shadows begin to shrink as time passed. The images that covered my path now disappeared as full light engulfs my surroundings. I also noticed the shadow cast of myself disappeared as the sun approached midday. How do I describe what I have just seen? What is the Holy Spirit revealing to me in the mystery of shadows?

The story revealed to me was a reminder of how the Old Testament cast shadows of God's ultimate plan as He allows the light of His Son to be present as mankind struggled to fulfill the requirements of the law given to Moses. In the New Testament I see Jesus in the flesh described as the light if the world. I see the shadows of the Old Testament disappear as Jesus walked the earth, died on the cross, was buried in a tomb, was resurrected from the dead, and ascended into heaven, thus initiating God's ultimate plan to make man one with Him.

As I translate this story, I see myself as an object that will produce a shadow when light is present. I know that Jesus is the light that resides within me as the Father placed the spirit of His Son within me the moment He birthed me as His son. As I saw the Son being a part of the shadows viewed today, I desire that all with whom I come in contact see the Light that forms the image of who I am. My desire is not to produce a shadow that is dimly seen, but rather to be totally surrendered to Him so that His light emanates through me as the midday Son. Thank you, Jesus, for speaking to me through the shadows today.

Sunrise at Toad River

Day dawns as the darkness flees with the first rays of light. The lake before me lies still as it prepares to reflect the glory of God, reminding all of His presence as His appearing illuminates the surrounding landscape. Anxious expectations arise within me as I wait in awestruck wonder to experience the magnificence of another day's beginning. The Creator has placed me in a new setting to reveal Himself as He paints a masterpiece of the beauty created for all to enjoy.

As the first rays of light appears over the eastern mountain range, a beautiful pink hue transforms a mountain peak before me, creating a spectacle my eyes had never witnessed. The scene captivates my imagination as images are formed upon the lake.

The lake is without a ripple on its surface as it reflects the beauty surrounding its boundary. The meadow in the distance appears on the surface. Nearby, the evergreen and aspens emerge to enhance the surface. A beaver's home appears as its occupants rest in quietness observing the spectacle while waiting for a day of labor. Two white swans sit motionless on the lake's surface, as if in reverence to the dawning of a new day. The fire weed and other plants are at attention, lifting arms of praise to our Lord. I stand, blessed to be able enjoy the wonder of creation.

I have waited, listened, and viewed a sunrise that surpasses my wildest dreams. As I continue to gaze at the surrounding beauty, the unclouded blue sky, the pink-hued mountain, the magnificent reflections upon the lake, the worship by creatures, and the praise of plants, I ask, what does this mean? The Lord reminded me that I was His son and He enjoyed revealing Himself to me in this manner. He wants me to remember this dawning and reflect upon His glory, and to realize He is always with me regardless of my location. What a wonderful dawning, what a cherished word, what a wonderful Father. I am so thankful to be His son, as a beautiful dawn puts life's essentials in the right perspective.

The Blessings Of Ma's Hands

When I think of Ma's hands, I am reminded of the fruits of the Spirit that were evident in her life. Her small hands were really a true expression of her heart. In my remembrance the appearance of her hands were small and dotted with the spots of age. They were delicate and not disfigured by disease. Her hands defined a lifetime of hard work and nurturing care for her ten children. Most people who knew Ma for very long seemed to recognize that her hands expressed the struggles of a simple life, the strength of a determined soul, and an expression of joy and love to all who were touched by her hands.

Physically, I saw Ma's hands performing unbelievable tasks, and yet with a touch so tender that she would amaze even a small child. I remember vividly her hands gripping the neck of a chicken and whirling it around until the head was all that remained in her hand. I have retained the memory of her hands as they washed dishes in an old battered dishpan. I can still hear her squeeze the dish cloth dry as water dripped from her fingers. Her hands could craft useful objects out of simple materials, such as Christmas ornaments, paper dolls, holiday surprises and birthday gifts. I can still see the care she used as she used her hands to knead the dough for her perfect biscuits. How I would love having some of her flat bread to satisfy my appetite. I still visualize her hands sifting through a lap full of green beans as she would break them to be canned for winter. It was fascinating to watch as Ma worked to prepare butter. She would take the butter out of the butter molds and with her hands she would carefully shape a beautiful cake of butter that would impress the most astute craftsman. With her hands, she could create beautiful clothing for her children, as the sewing needle seemed to work magic with each stitch.

I can only imagine how she would care for her children. I can only speculate on how those small hands would tenderly caress each infant child, how she would touch each feature while offering a prayer for the child's future. I can see her proudly admiring each child as her fingers would form a perfect curl in their hair. With amazement I think of how her hands were used to change and wash dozens of dirty diapers. She would wash them on a scrub board until they were without a spot hanging on the clothesline. I know there must have been comfort brought to each child as they were held in Ma's hands. Yes, Ma's hands were nurturing hands that brought love, joy, hope, and confidence to each child. I recall as a small child how she would take me by the hand and lead me to the garden with a spring in her step and a song on her lips. I could feel the love and security that flowed through her hands to me. Yes, Ma's hands could be described as nurturing hands.

Yet, as I have tried to paint a picture of Ma's hands of labor and nurture, Ma's hands seem to be admired as beautiful hands. Her hands were small and dainty. They possessed a natural beauty without the modern aids to enhance their appearance. They were a creation of the Lord as an extension of His life. Her hands were soft, which formed a disguise of the strength that was hidden from view. Her hands would be in constant motion as she would relate a story or tease us with a riddle. Her hands became a legend because everyone remembers the touch of Ma's hands.

As I began, I described Ma's hands as the fruits of the Spirit. I was blessed to feel the love expressed by the touch of her hands as I felt special to her. I remember the joy expressed in her hands as she would sing or speak of happy times. I can visualize long-suffering in her hands, as she related stories of her trials and tribulations. I have been touched by the kindness in her hands as she cared for those in need. Peace was present in her hands as the touch would calm many fears. She was gifted with gentleness in her hands that radiated from her very being. There was faithfulness in her hands as she gripped the hand of the one she loved as a lifelong mate. Yes, there was a goodness present in Ma's hands, which was evident to everyone who knew her.

In describing Ma's hands, I have written that they were an extension of who she really was to me. With her hands she was able to express the love of God to many people. I realize that I am a better person because the Lord allowed me to be touched by Ma's hands. Many expressions of Ma's hands I did not pen, but the reality of the impact of her hands on those who knew her will forever be brought to mind. I look forward to the day when, as one of the Lord's chosen, I will be able to reach out and once again know the touch of Ma's hands.

The Call Of The Mountains

Micah 4:2 *"Come let us go up to the mountain of the Lord, and to the house of Jacob: that He may teach us His ways, and that we may walk in His paths,"*

As I set my eyes upon the mountains, a voice inside me seems to be saying, "come to me, come and see." The yearning to go is irresistible as I scan the magnificence of these wonders of nature. The beckoning call seems to intensify as I wonder why the call to go is so great. Is it the pleasure of escaping the world's problems to find comfort in solitude? Is it the quest to discover hidden mysteries of historical significance? Is it the beauty to be enjoyed as the seasons come and go? Could it possibly be to a place where I can experience a life-changing moment, as I encounter One on one the creator of the universe? Only by my presence in the mountains will the answer be revealed to satisfy my curiosity. So I must go.

I venture into the mountains at the dawning of a new day. I am greeted with a sense of stillness as only the sound of my footsteps crunching the fallen leaves can be heard. A quiet reverence surrounded me as I entered the sacred grounds. Awe grips my soul as the rays of morning sunlight beam through the morning mist, creating images that challenge my creative thoughts. A sparkle of joy bursts forth as the light of day dances on the foliage of massive trees, witnessing history etching its story. I notice beautiful wildflowers waking, with blooms reaching heavenward—giving thanks for a peaceful night and proclaiming the glory of a new day. I happen upon a trail representing a destination unknown to me, but a revelation of the mystery of man's curiosity as I journey on this path.

My journey encounters many trails that cut through the mountain terrain. I wonder, who planned these trails? Or were they planned at all? They led me by streams of water, seeming to be singing a lullaby as they tumbled over the rocky formations that rose from the earth. I hiked through flower-laden laurel thickets and rocky inclines that weep as if saddened by their existence. The trail led me through a mesa where animals could be seen forging for food. I walked by caves that served as shelters for man and beast. As I pressed onward, I was astonished to see the remains of bygone days, as only a foundation or a chimney remained of a home that once housed the happiness of a family. Cemeteries emerged that were the final resting place of the young and old when times were primitive. I was finally blessed to visit the mountaintop, where views defied description and expanded to the distant horizon. Yes, these were where life's greatest moments could be revisited.

My day in the mountains draws to an end as hues of red clouds reflect the setting of the sun. A gentle breeze begins to whisper through the forest, thus birthing an inspiration of thanksgiving in me for the opportunities I experienced. The trees clapping, the flowers bowing, the birds singing expressed the joy found by my visitation.

These closing events ushered in thoughts of my Savior. He went to the mountains to pray. He preached a great sermon on a mount. He went to Mount Calvary to die as me for my sins and give His life in exchange for my life of darkness. He ascended to heaven from a mountain and will return to earth on the same mountain. I did discover solitude in the mountains. I was privileged to reminisce with history. Beauty was found in an abundant supply. I was blessed to experience life-changing moments as I found pleasure in my venture with just Jesus and me. The mountains said come and see, so I went and saw. He taught me His ways and I now walk on His paths.

The Epitome Of Joy

R ecently, as I was attempting to photograph a butterfly seeking nectar from a flaming azalea, waves of joy began to flood my thinking process. These thought revelations seemed to intensify as I witnessed in awestruck wonder the movements of the butterfly. The seeming ease with which the creature darted, danced, elevated, and lowered itself brought a bounty of pleasure to me as the insect fluttered through its daily routine. I questioned why I sensed such joy in the presence of a butterfly. A beautiful creature it was, but really, could a butterfly carry and share a gift of joy? It deserved further study.

The life of a butterfly has a meager and inauspicious beginning. Erupting from an egg laid by a female parent, a larva emerges and is nourished as it feeds on the foliage of plants. As the larva grows, the appearance of a caterpillar evolves. Beauty is not the word to describe this creature. In fact, the appearance is so distasteful that ending its life is foremost in the thoughts of many humans. As the caterpillar continues to grow, life becomes more perilous as predators are more prevalent.

So what are the thoughts of this ugly woolen critter relegated to crawl to each destination as it seeks sustenance to sustain its existence? Many thoughts arise in his mind as the life process continues. Thoughts of fear surface, as a defense in the face of danger is limited. Putting myself in his place, the idea that this is my destiny creates a sense of hopelessness for my purpose in life. Sensing I was created to always crawl on the ground is nagging at my happiness. In my heart, many questions arise regarding who and why I am. As I gaze into heaven, I dream of how wonderful it must be to fly. I look at my appearance and realize my dream is likely just a dream. How could I possibly change myself? After all, it takes all of my effort to just stay alive and avoid the pitfalls I face. Even so, something in my inner being tells me I am not who I am meant to be. Am I a mistake, or am I in some way confused? Unhappiness reigns in me as I have questions needing an answer. Distancing myself from my present surroundings seems to be the only option I have to discover the answer to my longings. To rid myself of the ever-present distractions of life, I will enclose myself in a secluded place until I find relief in the quest of who I am in the eyes of my Creator. Maybe His definition of who I am is different from what I have experienced.

As I was alone for a period of time in silent solitude, I confessed that I was not who I was supposed to be, and I was not happy existing in a world of fear and chaos. In desperation, I began pleading with my Creator to share with me the reasons my feelings seemed to be in contradiction to the life I was living. He answered and said, "If you will trust Me, I will recreate you into a new creature I desire you to be. You will be a new creation, old things will pass away and behold all things will become new to you." I readily replied to Him, "I do trust you." Instantly I noticed light entering my darkness and illuminating my surroundings. As I was beginning to emerge from my enclosure,

I looked at my body and noticed I had wings. Wow, I now have the capability to fly, a deep-seated desire could now be satisfied as I will be able to reach all the destinations planned for me. I am blessed with a new body, arrayed with clothing of joy and peace. I have been given a new name to the delight of my Maker. I can now be a beacon of hope for others, who are still in the crawling stage of life, as I flit from flower to flower enjoying the sweetness of a changed life. What a love my Creator has for me, to change me to satisfy His ultimate intention for me. I am so thankful. My soul is flooded with joy. My desire now is for the world to witness the joy I radiate. I am so happy to be a new creation.

As I consider the life of a butterfly, I see an expression of the life of Christ in me. The joy within me is real and not conjured up by my feeble effort. Much like the butterfly, the question of who I am needed to be answered. A yearning within me amplified the need for His presence to complete the ultimate intention He had for me. My efforts were futile as I tried unsuccessfully to answer the question within the realm of my human existence. A rebirth was necessary for me to be transformed into the creature the Father could accept as his son. Jesus was placed in me and I became a part of the new creation race. My life is now eternal with Him. I have a hope living within me, a peace is present, love is my greatest gift, and joy is without boundaries. What a privilege to be a completed son in Jesus and to have a Father who loves me as I am. Thanks little butterfly for reminding me of this great gift. Thank you, Father, for adopting me to be your joy-filled son.

The Gift Of Light

So many blessings I have taken for granted, leaving me with a feeling that gratitude has been missing in every expression of my life. This morning I began the day by meditating on the gift of light. As the morning dawns, I am aware that the cloud of darkness, which had engulfed me during my restful slumber, is fading as the first glimmer of light emerges. My thoughts are now guided to my visible surroundings, which had been hidden from my sight, but now have been illuminated by the presence of light.

My mental capacity is overwhelmed as I focus on the source of light, essential to view the sights that encompass my presence. I am suddenly conscious of a phenomenon the author of creation is unfolding. In His wisdom, He placed the sun in the heavens to beam light to the earth. This light provides a medium by which I see, a warmth for my comfort, and a necessary ingredient for a healthy existence. His mighty work is on daily display as he commands the sun to perform its duty according to His plan.

I witness the first rays of sunlight as they pattern a path from the earth to the outer regions of the universe in my imagination. I stand in awe as the sun rises over the eastern mountaintops and illuminates the valleys below. I see clouds come alive as hues of red, pink, orange and golden color bring breathtaking moments into view. I see the dew-drenched ground sparkle as the light enters its presence. I am amazed as I witness the petals of flowers open their arms to embrace the warmth of light's new appearance. Babbling brooks bounce to and fro, now able to reflect all the images that appear upon their surface. I watch nocturnal creatures scampering to their hidden dens, as if fear of the deeds done in darkness may be exposed.

As I think of the morning sunrise and the first light of day, I am reminded of what must have been the most indescribable sight as witnessed from heaven. I wonder what emotions God experienced as the first sunrise awakened the earth after creation was finished. I am sure He was delighted when He saw that darkness on earth was now subject to the light of day. I can not find words to print, nor can my mind imagine the beauty of the earth as viewed from heaven, when life as we know it was only an infant.

My musings are now challenged as I turn to another part of the day. The sun begins to settle down in the depths of the horizon, departing in a blaze of brilliance that captivates my attention. Its presence disappears and silence prevails, as the beauty of its exit rivals the splendor of its entrance. God in his infinite wisdom brings forth a reflection of the sun to meet my needs even in the darkest hours of day. He placed the moon high above to be a reflector of the light of life. Within the moon He placed the power to control the mighty seas, which are often capable of a raging fury, bringing a destructive force unimaginable to man. He places stars throughout the heavens knowing them all by name creating a canopy of light that has often baffled the most intellectual thoughts of man. The stars have frequently provided direction for lost wayfarers and served as guiding lights for confused captains upon a stormy sea, all the while proclaiming the glory of God.

The created beauty of earth was marred, as sin and death invaded the heart of man and darkness penetrated his soul. Darkness again prevailed upon the earth as man stumbled in disobedience. But God in His far-reaching mercy sent another "Son rise" to rescue man from his darkness. His name is Jesus. He left the splendor of heaven to inhabit the earth as the light of the world. He suffered on a cruel cross until death. He was buried in a cold tomb, and arose three days later to erase the hopelessness that surrounded man in his darkness. He was placed in man, and man in Him, for all who would believe in Him. Man is now able, because of this union, to become the light in a dark world.

As I reminisce, I inquire of Him what His eternal intention is for me as His son in this journey of life. Is He instructing me in ways that mirror His image? Is He revealing Himself to me in ways I have not imagined? As He seeks new ways to relate to me, is He really exposing all that He is in me? Will His purpose be consummated in me as the glory of His light glows from my inner man? As I conclude, His Son is still shining from within believing man to usher forth His glory to His satisfaction.

Yes, I have been transformed out of darkness into light. As the sunrise extends its rays to expose the beauty of God's creation, so I shine forth the rays He created out of darkness to magnify the beauty of His Son, Jesus. As the light emanates out of my being, I am able to lift up the fallen, to give sight to the blind, to give hope to the despairing, to comfort those in need, and to proclaim the wonderful truths of our

Lord Jesus. My path is illuminated by His word. My darkness has been defeated by the cross. My future has been determined by His grace. My walk is guarded by His Spirit, and my boasting is in His glory. His intention for me is that I be a reflection of His glory. I am so grateful that He chose to shine His light upon me and now may I be found guilty of allowing His light to shine forth out of me, a rescued slave of darkness.

The Legacy of the Sailboat

The journey of life can be personified as a sailboat that navigates the challenges presented to her upon the sea of life. My story begins as I visualize an old sailboat biding her time in the dry docks of the harbor of rest. She is safely and securely moored with only the memories of bygone adventures that defined her life. I was saddened to see her once admired body had been robbed of it's beauty. Her once brilliant white hull had turned gray with streams of rust stains streaking toward the water below. Her once proud sails are now tattered as if they had lost the battle with the elements of nature. They are rolled up in a heap, without form, serving only as an occasional perch for a tired, weary seagull. Her keel reveals the age marks of mildew and decay, from the many years of contact with the briny waters of the deep. Her once proud deck seemed antiquated when compared to present versions.

As I have described, her appearance no longer attracts much attention, yet her beauty seems to radiate from within, as memories are laced within her cabin waiting to be shared with any curious stranger.

Today I wandered into the depths of her cabin to listen to the story she was yearning to share. She speaks of her birth when she was brought into existence by her maker.

She was nurtured with the greatest of care as each part was assembled and neatly joined together, reflecting the work of a master craftsman. After days of preparation, her time to sail occupied her thought process. She relates how the burning desire of her youth was to launch out on the sea and experience the adventure that lay before her.

Her tall mast towered toward heaven, adorned with fluttering white sails ready to test the gentle breeze. Her beautiful wood-garnished cabin is ready to entertain her first guest and to be admired as a work of art by her creator. Her bronze-laden helm is to be grasped by her helmsman who is prepared to guide her path over life's sea.

As her maiden voyage begins, great excitement reigns as spectators wish her well. Cheers fill the air as she is launched on this beautiful spring morning. The invisible Creator of all seemed to express His approval as He offered a setting too magnificent to verbalize adequately. The morning sun is rising with the heavenly blue sky in the background. The silky white clouds dance in the sky, producing formations that mystify the imagination. A gentle breeze arrives to carry her over the glassy calm waters of the bay, while playful whitecaps ripple in the distance. She skims joyfully along with the grace of a swan as she begins her journey of life.

Her journey included many experiences, which she graciously shared as I sat, spell-bound, listening to each word she uttered about the joys and trials of her story. She shared with a sparkle in her eyes the joy and happiness she had while seas were calm and danger seemed non-existent. Stories of joy she related included showing hospitality to all who desired her presence. She glowingly shared the excitement of the multitudes that walked upon her deck, to experiencing the grandeur present in the panoramic beauty of the sea. She shared with thanksgiving that many of her hopes and dreams were fulfilled as she ventured across the inviting sea. She somberly related experiences with tear-stained eyes of the many battles she confronted against the raging sea.

The stories of gale-force winds amidst dark storm clouds and lighting dancing near her bow tempting her to alter her course. She had praise for her captain, who steered her though the raging tide, knowing the chosen course would test her strength to overcome the fear she felt. Her body would tremble under the force of pressure generated by a menacing sea. Her desire to continue would come into question, and her motivation to overcome would wane.

How could she outlast such pressure? How would she be able to weather the storm? Had she been weakened to the point of compromise? The answer would lie in her resolve to persevere, inspired by the spirit within her and the constant encouraging words of her captain.

Yes, another temptation had been overcome and her virtue remained. And the battle of life's storms continued. She shared how, among many stressful battles with despair and hopelessness surrounding her, in the center of a storm she would strain to see the beacon of a lighthouse on the horizon, knowing once again, this trial would be overcome and her future preserved.

She told many stories as I listened intently. Some were happy, some were sad, some humorous, some seriously true, and all were important to weave her story of life. As I analyzed her story, I saw Jesus as her captain, who sailed life's journey with her. I saw the gentle breeze as the Holy Spirit who empowered her through life. I saw the lighthouse as God's presence beckoning her to Him for her eternal rest. Yes, she now rests in the harbor never to sail again. Her testimony has much to teach me about the battles of life. The wisdom I acquired included the joys of triumph, the sorrow of disappointments, hope in the trials, and the endurance to continue. I have learned to put my trust in the captain, to listen to the gentle breeze, and to look expectantly to basking in the lighthouse of my Father's presence.

As I slowly left her presence with an occasional glance over my shoulder, not really wanting to leave, I pondered her words and my body trembled as I realized her story sounded so strangely familiar. As I reached the crest of the hill overlooking the harbor, my parting words would be thank you, graceful lady, for sharing your story with me, another sailor on the sea of life. You have touched my heart today, as I penned your story with tear-filled eyes.

The River

"There is a river, the streams whereof shall make glad the city of God" Psalms 46:4

Streams are birthed into existence without the influence of man. Their origins can only be traced to the Creator of the universe. The streams began as love, flowing from the heart of God in the form of raindrops of love, mercy, and grace. They were redeemed and cleansed as the Creator sacrificed His Son. His blood now covers the streams with a crimson stain. The streams are sustained as the showers of His Holy Spirit give refreshing new life, power, and purpose to each stream.

The streams begin small and shallow and tend to move swiftly as they search for meaning, for the revelation of who they are in life. As they seek for the purpose of their existence, they tend to be easily diverted, and their original course altered. Fruitless energy is spent in seeking the way in which they can flow without resistance, but the resistance has to be overcome for the water to become the pure, clear, unadulterated streams they were created to be.

In the course of their flow, the appearance of some of the streams seem destined to change. Some streams become muddy as a result of the struggle for their identity. Some streams become cloudy as a result of having to compromise in their weakness. Some streams become polluted because of their direction of flow through the world. Some streams become stagnant from separating from the source that sustains their existence, and become independent as to their direction of flow. Regardless of their appearances, all streams are important in the creation and ultimate purpose of the river.

Some streams flow freely, enthusiastically from the mountaintops with little resistance. Some flow through the beautiful meadows and lowly valleys where resistance is often hidden or disguised. Some streams tumble through the rapids of deep ravines, where trouble and distress seem to lurk with each movement. Some streams trickle to the desert where the heat of resistance makes their flow unbearable.

Amid the hardships of the flow, or the troubles encountered along the way, there is a yearning within the heart of each stream to reach her destination. The destination that has been prescribed by the Creator is inevitable; that is, the river, the sea, or evaporation into non-existence, each of which is a glorious reunion with the source from whence they came.

The river comprises many streams that have emptied themselves of their past and are now ready to flow in harmony with other streams toward a destination where they will further lose their identity. The river is deep and moves slowly as if almost at rest. The river receives all streams freely and without condemnation. The river receives purity from the crystal clear stream. She receives the struggle of self-effort from the muddy stream. She receives the weakness of indecision from the cloudy stream. She receives the hurts of independence from the stagnant stream. The river receives the failures of life from the polluted stream. Impossible as it may seem, the river gladly receives from each and all streams, and as a result of her willingness to receive, the river's purpose bursts forth in life with all that she touches.

The river flows harmoniously, as the streams, which make up her very being, experience a change in appearance and character. No stream desires to be known as the largest part of the river. No stream acts independently of the other streams. No stream claims to have all knowledge of all truth. No stream pursues the elevation of self. All streams within the river are focused on one destination, union with the sea. As the river flows and fulfills her purpose, a great excitement and expectancy is generated; a peace is observed, a joy is expressed, and love is abounding at limitless heights. What an indescribable marriage will take place when the river is finally, once and for all time, united with the sea.

As the God of the universe has personified through nature the purposes for the streams and rivers, He also has illustrated His desire for His glorious church, the Bride of His Son, Jesus.

Yes, "There is a river the streams whereof make glad the city of God" (Ps. 46:4). It's a river with her origin in the heart of God, her birth in the Son of God, and her sustaining flow in the Spirit of God. May the river bring life, joy and peace to everything she touches until that great wedding day.

The Rocker

As I sit in this rickety old rocker, I am flooded with memories of a bygone life. I am overcome with wonderful thoughts of my grandparents, known to me as Pa and Ma. I see them living in the simplicity of life in their time. I see Pa sitting in this old rocker with a pipe in his mouth and a newspaper held by both hands hiding his face as he reads. While sitting by the fire, I could see a trickle of smoke rising above the newspaper and smell the aroma of pipe smoke as it filled the air. A cough would emerge as Pa cleared his throat, and the newspaper would noisily come together as he turned from page to page. I often wondered what this quiet hard-working man was thinking. I know this old rocker was where he spent a lot of time reading, thinking, planning, resting, and I believe, praying for his own. I recall the crackling sound the rocker made on the old wood floor as it was propelled by the grand old man who occupied it.

I see Ma taking a break during her busy day to sit in this old rocker with an apron filled with freshly picked green beans. Ma would sit and rock as she broke the beans to prepare for an evening meal. Ma never seemed to grow tired or weary. Somehow she would press on with timeless energy. Some of my fondest memories of Ma were when the supper dishes were finished. She would sit in this old rocker, draw a deep sigh of relief, and expect relief to come from a hard day's work. Yet with a twinkle in her eye, she would find great pleasure when I, as an eager child, would sit near her and ask her to tell me a story or relate a riddle to me that I could try to solve. Ma lived a life of simplicity knowing people mattered more than things. It was a life that required a great amount of effort to survive, but still she had time at the end of the day to bring pleasure to me as I sat at her feet. Yes, I have fond memories of the two people who once occupied this old chair. They deeply touched my life. The old rocker is a constant reminder to me of their blessed life. The chair shows the stress of time, but if it could speak I am sure it would express pride in the ones who found comfort as they rocked, rested, prayed, and found delight in the life they lived.

There Will Never Be Another Sunset Quite Like This One

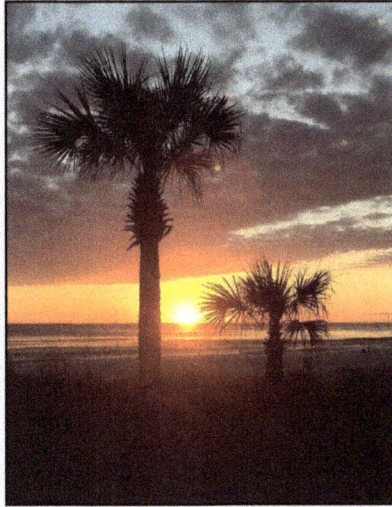

D ay is done, the labors of the day are approaching a historical climax. Our busyness has engulfed us, our thoughts of a hectic day enthrall us, and the haste with which we drive home is met with snarling traffic. We glance skyward and see airplanes streaking toward their destinations, crowded with weary travelers. At home, we encounter the frustrations of trying to prepare a meal for all the family, whose interests carry them in many directions, such as, striving to meet obligations, fulfill a dream, or satisfy a longing. Yes, this seems to be a typical ending to an event-filled day with pressures lingering that will define the day. But on the horizon of the western sky, the brilliance of sunset offers a pleasant reminder of the blessings of life we encounter by the mere privilege of living this day. As the final moments of day approach, a thought resonates within us that there will never be another sunset quite like this one.

As the sun begins to sink into the earth's horizon, the Creator of the universe steps to the platform of His cosmic creation to orchestrate a majestic ending to another day. The instruments are fine-tuned, the string section is about to send forth multicolor rays as only heaven can produce. The brass section is ready to embrace the moment with a triumphant approval, while the percussion section is ready thunder out an exclamation point of joy. Our Lord is ready, once again, to make Himself known through the beauty of a sunset of which there will never be another one quite like this one.

If we could only see the whole picture from God's view, we would stand in awe and marvel at the grandeur of each day's sunset. As we have noticed the struggle of mankind to peacefully traverse the day, we take note that nature is in a state of expectancy as the day approaches an end.

The mountains are standing tall as monuments to His glory. Some are laced with trees whose branches stretch forth toward heaven offering chords of praise, as a gentle breeze walks in their midst. Others are barren, but adorned with a garment of snow as they are dressed for the upcoming spectacle. The multitude of streams are flowing with a harmonic melody that only they can produce. The rivers are gliding with effortless ease toward their destinations. The oceans are clad with white-capped splendor as they race toward land. The sands of the deserts lie in silence waiting to reflect their beauty, which has been hidden by the scorching heat of the day. The fowls of the air and the animals of the land seem to sense that day is ending on a note that there will never be another one quite like this one.

The sun is drifting lower, the clouds of various shapes have taken their places. The Lord lifts His baton, while the orchestra snaps to attention to ring forth the symphonic sounds to begin the only performance exactly like this one. The baton waves, the strings sounds forth with perfect pitch sending brilliant red bands cascading through silky white clouds. The brass joins in under the direction of the Master's hand, causing the mountains to celebrate as the trees light up with breathless beauty with red and orange beams filtering through their foliage. The snow-capped mountains are illuminated with colors ranging from red to pink as the sun sets at various stages. The percussion sections sounds out notes that dispatch streams of golden rays that dance upon the waters of the earth. The whitecaps of the oceans come alive with a blazing array of color that paint a highway to the sun. Likewise, the streams and rivers dance onward clothed in colors that mystify viewers. The sands of the deserts sparkle with delight as tones of red and yellow inhabit their abandoned setting, creating a rainbow of colors that seem to bring life to the dormant landscape.

As the sun sinks deeper into the western horizon, the colors in the heavenly amphitheater begin to change from the awe-striking reds to a rapidly darkening gray, signaling the ending of a sunset that will never be repeated quite like this one. Mountain peaks stand in loneliness as darkness begins to veil the earth, the trees stand peacefully as if the night will bring rest, the streams and rivers flow with sounds that seem to amplify their grateful crescendo for the joy they just experienced. The ocean's whitecaps abate to a calmness that settles the earlier raging surf. The desert sands relax as a coolness in the air sweeps over her terrain. The flowers, whose beauty graced the day, now bow in humble appreciation for the evening sights they have just witnessed.

The Lord takes a bow while surrounded by the heavenly host on bended knee as they worship Him with joyful song, shouting forth praises to Him for what they were invited to experience. As He exits the platform and reminisces the magnificent production He has just directed, I wonder if He is disappointed that so many of His greatest creations fail to notice His handiwork? These are questions I ponder. But I know He has already answered my questions to His own satisfaction. Now for all of us who had the opportunity to witness this grand gift of love sent to us, I hope we took time to applaud His glory, because there will be another sunset quite like this one.

Touched By Heaven's Declaration

The heavens declare the glory of God and the sky proclaims His handiwork. (Ps. 19:1)

Recently as I was on my morning walk listening to the hymn, "Nearer My God to Thee," I cast my eyes into the sky above and experienced the awesome presence of the Lord. On this occasion, He seemed to want to reassure me of who I am in Him, and relate it to me in such a way that it would be permanently etched in my spirit. Normally when I walk, prayer, praise and worship consume my thoughts as I desire to exalt the Lord and His majesty.

This day was different because when I turned my eyes skyward I was awestruck by the sight and was certain God would use it to communicate a message to me. Before me was a cross created by the jet streams of aircraft streaking across the sky. The cross was fading and growing wider, and was swiftly losing its identity as a cross. I sensed the Lord was describing this cross as follows: this cross actually represents the payment required of you for your sin against me. The fact that this cross is fading away means the payment required of you was paid by Another Person.

As I continued my walk, I glanced toward the eastern sky and viewed a more defined cross silhouetted against an expanse of clear blue sky. The Lord described this cross as the one Jesus died upon as me, to satisfy the debt I owed for my sin. Tears filled my eyes as thanksgiving flooded my being. It was as if I could feel the drops of blood dripping from that cross as I walked beneath. I looked beyond to the beauty of a blue sky; it was as if the Lord was saying, "This is my glory being declared."

I then directed my attention to the south, behind me. I witnessed dark storm clouds gathering above the distant mountain range. In front of the clouds was an X formed also by the jet streams. The message I sensed in my heart was that this display represented who I use to be-a slave to darkness. The X meant my concern for my sins of the past should no longer haunt me because Jesus death for me had made them a non-issue. I am no longer to be condemned by my past, but to rejoice in my freedom as a son of God.

What joy flooded my heart as I continued home, reassured once more that I am complete in Him. I have often expressed in jest, that if God would only write a message to me in the sky, it would be much easier for me. Today, He granted me that desire. As I have thought about this experience, I know the Lord chose these illustrations so I could experience His infinite love for me. I realize it was not just happenstance that aircraft formed this message for me, but rather I know it was His handiwork in the sky to encourage me on my journey. Yes the heavens declare His glory. The blue expanse of the sky, the numerous cloud formations, sunrises, sunsets, moon and stars daily broadcast the beauty of His holiness. I was so blessed to witness this proclamation as I experienced "Nearer My God to Thee" first hand.

Beauty in the Valley of Life

Life is often described in terms that personify mountains and valleys as expressions of life's experiences. But as I ponder the life I have lived and experiences that have molded me, I have to admit that life in the valley is where I seem to have spent the most time, and rather than being punishing, it is often filled with beauty as well as lessons. It has been an adventure, filled with danger, struggles, battles, and conflicts which have produced victories to my soul that surpass any thoughts of failure that may surface when reminiscing life in the valley. Although the valley is filled with many obstacles to overcome, such as doubt, darkness, hurt, temptation, and sickness; life in the valley is the schoolhouse where we are made ready for our heavenly entrance.

Life and beauty in the valley have taken on various personalities as I review the events that have taken place in the valleys of my life. I have been so amazed by sights that words are not available to describe in valleys where the sky seems to touch the meadow below where an array of colorful vegetation would be reaching to welcome it's presence. I have walked on valley floors where the deer bounded nearby as they playfully traveled to new feeding grounds. I have experienced the beauty of the valley when a sunset brought cascades of color as hues of pink and scarlet illuminated the sky and reflecting on the landscape as if from the brush of a master artist. I have been touched as I roamed through the valley's meadows at daybreak and found landscape aglow as glistening dew drops brought refreshment to the petals of daisies, buttercups, and dandelions. Nothing is more beautiful to me than a stream tumbling through the valley floor bringing nourishment to everything it touches as it travels toward it's destination. The scene of animals grazing in the distant fields has brought a sense of serenity and harmony without a threat of lurking danger.

All is not pleasant in the valley, as I have been present when darkness would descend and I would be engulfed with loneliness and fear. As danger would appear to be more imminent yet all would be cleared away as I would notice the heavens were ablaze with the lights skillfully placed by our Creator. I have walked in valleys where only memories remain of life's past struggles. I have been in valleys where graveyards dot the land where young and old alike were ravaged by disease. I have visited valleys where freedom battles were fought and old cannons survived to relate part of the story of the struggle. The struggles to defend man's ideals, where their passions were played out, and pain and death were apparent as man sought victory in the valley.

As I have briefly portrayed the valley in natural terms, a spiritual thought is born. In the valley in times of meditation, I realize that life's dreams and visions were birthed, that disappointments and challenges were encountered, and that the battle rages on as life struggles for victory. I have walked through the valley of the shadow of death on two memorable occasions only to be victorious by the touch of God's hand. I have experienced failure. I have been acquainted with grief yet consoled by God's goodness. I know what it is like not to have a passing grade and not be able to pay my bills in a timely manner, yet God's abundant blessings vanished those thoughts. I have experienced hurt from a close friend and yet God removed all bitterness. I have felt the loneliness of trying to solve problems alone, but God would assure me that He would never leave or forsake me. I have been torn by doubt, despair, depression, guilt, and shame but God's promises restored me. I have experienced love, joy, peace, and an outpouring of God's abundance in my walk through the valley. I've experienced many more victories as life in the valley continues. Most of all, God's grace has allowed me to conquer life's greatest foes. When I accepted the Lord's call to be His child, death was defeated and everlasting life with Him was born. All other victories pale in comparison to the grace granted to me when His blood covered all my sins to be remembered no more. The largest giant I face has fallen. Yes, victory is possible in the valley of life with God fighting the battles with me.

What a Wonderful Thought

Early this morning, I was awakened by a most wonderful thought passing through my semi-conscious state. The thought consisted of an old truth that I had been taught and yet a freshness of its reality seemed to flood my soul. The phrase *you are a completed work of grace* seemed to be enhanced to a new level of understanding as I pondered the magnitude of the phrase.

As I lay basking in the renewed revelation, the only expression that would define my feelings was, what a wonderful thought. What a way to begin to begin the day. What joy seemed to ooze through my being. Peace began to gather in my soul. Abundant love expressed to me existed to make this thought surface from concept to reality. Yes, my emotions danced as I seemed to be enthralled by the finality of the meaning of a completed work of grace.

My thoughts seemed to span the entire existence of my lifetime. Thoughts of my early childhood, when I was being wooed by the Holy Spirit through my love for invitational hymns. When I accepted His choosing of me, I had no idea that I had experienced the completion of grace at that very moment. I began to think of my youthful years when I was protected by His presence. Images of my middle-aged years were re-lived as He graced me with my precious family.

My thoughts began to center on the present, as He prepares me for the glorification of a completed work of grace. I look at the fragile housing that I walk around in daily. I notice the wrinkles of time rippling through most of my body. I see silver-laced hair, and skin dotted with various spots and growths. I feel energy waning and body parts in need of repair. And yet, I realize what I am actually viewing is the image of God whom He created me to be.

This body has housed me well for three score and ten years. It also houses my Lord Jesus, as I was somehow placed in Him at the time of my rebirth to make me worthy to be called a joint-heir, a son of my Heavenly Father, though still flawed by the ravages of sin that exist in my flesh.

As I continue my thoughts, my attention is once again focused on the cross, the instrument on which Jesus suffered and died for me. How could He endure such pain and agony? How is it possible that 2000 years ago the blood He shed formed a crimson-stained river that would flow through the ages, and cleanse me of all my sin? How could He love me that much? Questions I can never answer, but the explanation will always entertain my desires to know.

I have expressed a few of my thoughts; so what have I learned? I have learned anew not to be anxious about tomorrow. I am reminded of the high price of forgiveness paid for me. I know that where Jesus is, I am there also. I know that when I disappoint Him, He is not surprised, but ready to remind me of His blood-stained sacrifice for me.

I have enjoyed the day, and have been blessed by His reminder that I am a completed work of grace. What a wonderful thought to start the day. May I never doubt the work of grace performed in me. How can I express or explain grace? I cannot in the fullest extent, but I know it is the tool created by a loving Father to bring me into eternal existence with Him, which is more than enough to explain the completed work of grace in me. My praises are directed to honor Jesus, who thought enough of me to quicken my spirit, as I began this day with this most wonderful thought.

Path of Hope

Proverbs 4:18. *The path of the righteous is like the first gleam of dawn, which shines ever brighter until the full light of day. (NLT)*

As I thought about the paths that I have walked, they are all different as I visualize their physical description. I have walked on paths that were so worn that the dirt would be viewed as slick. Some paths were leaf-covered so densely that you could hardly find your way. Some have been covered with gravel. Some were paved with asphalt or concrete, while some were etched out of sand, and still others traced through streams. The paths would always have an origin and a destination.

I have hiked on paths across mountaintops with views of grandeur as I would gaze at the vistas far and near. I have traveled on paths that followed mountain streams that produced a language spoken by nature, as the streams babbled over the rock-filled terrain. Strolling on paths of sand by the ocean, I experienced the gentle breeze and was mystified by the pounding surf. I have raced on paths that led to childhood excitement as the destination would be a sandlot ball field or a secret hideout. I have walked on paths where I never found the end, as they seemed to go on forever. I have walked on paths that have been traveled for hundreds of years and yet still provide a passage for the present.

On some paths it seemed not a sound could be heard and only the throes of loneliness would be felt. I have hiked on paths through meadows that screamed out beauty with a flowering spring. I have traveled paths covered with snow that brought a stillness to my soul, only to be disturbed by the crunching of my feet upon the snow. I have hiked paths beside lakes which boasted the splendor of fall with the reflection of a collection of painted foliage upon its surface. I have been present on trails that were not adequately visible and experienced the apprehension of being lost surface in my inner being. I have hiked mountainous paths that produced fear just by the nature and appearance of the path, as danger seemed to be lurking at any moment. In these moments, my walk would quickly turn into a run.

As you can see, I have many visions of paths that can be recalled and described. Yet who would imagine the path I travel would be so rewarding, since I share this path with so many others on the same journey? People from all walks of life from near and far with varied backgrounds and spiritual experiences. We travel the same path and are blessed by discovering we are walking the same path, as we share our oneness with each other. Yes, as our paths have crossed and met, we understand that really we have been walking the same path for a number of years. My description of the path we are traveling is best described as "The Path of Hope." This path is filled with many awesome sights. As I look back on the path that I have traveled, I see so many pitfalls, so many side paths, dangers, and snares. There have been so many disappointments, hatred, injustice, and unfairness. So much sin, so much happiness, so much love, and so much mercy. And most of all, a path brightened by Grace.

I was placed on my path before I knew of what a path consisted. Before my birth my path of purpose was planned by the One in whose footsteps I was to follow. Yes, this path had been trodden long ago by the One who began this path from a garden and paved it through the ages. It culminates in a city more glorious than words are adequate to describe.

I accepted the invitation to walk the path of hope at a young age. I accepted because of a strong drawing and yearning to walk a path, which at the time I did not fully understand. Also, to my surprise, I was given a Guide for the journey Who had traveled the entire length of the path many times. His name was Lord Jesus. Little did I know how eager He was to show me the way, to warn me of danger, and would be willing to rescue me when I would stray from the path.

As I look back, I ask the question, "was this the easiest path to walk?" I have to answer no. How could I have known what was before me on this path? I have had path experiences that have taken me to mountaintops, through lovely meadows, and by streams that tumble across a thirsty land bringing floods of joy to my soul as I experienced my Savior's love, and realized that I was pleasing to Him. Still aware of these precious moments, I would still wander down the path of temptation, which constantly zigzagged across the path of hope. It was in these times that pleasure and self-gratification entered through wrong choices. Almost immediately the feeling of guilt, shame, and loneliness were present to torment me. The still small voice of my Guide would beckon me back to the right path, and through repentance the journey would continue.

This has been a glorious walk so far, filled with every emotion I possess. There have been times when my Guide and I walked side by side, and other times I followed in His footsteps. At times He had to carry me over raging currents. There were occasions when I felt surrounded as if the path ran through a box canyon and He had to lead me out. There are times when the attacks by the fearful enemy are more than I can bear, but He says, I have overcome him, fear not. There are times when I worry and fret about the direction of the path, but He comforts me with His abiding presence as we rest beside a calming brook. Through all my trials and frustrations I have experienced as I journey along this path, my Guide has never complained or refused to extend His hand of grace. He has promised as I walk this path that He will never leave or forsake me and I have nothing to fear.

Finally, as I gaze toward the end of the path, I see the mountains before me silhouetted on the horizon, aglow with the lights of that city, which define the end of His predetermined path. What a blessing to walk His path in His presence. What a wonderful trip. What a wonderful hope. What a wonderful Jesus.

Crossing the Bridge

As I approached the bridge this morning—I realized I was receiving a message as I viewed the scene before me.

As I neared the bridge, I noticed I was walking in darkness provided by the tree-lined trail, while on the other side of the bridge the sun was brightly illuminating the path. I saw the bridge spanning the creek as Jesus laying down his life and becoming the bridge that could lead me from my darkness to the light and presence of His Father. As I contemplated crossing the bridge, He told me if I would trust Him, He would introduce me to His Father. So I put my trust in Him and He imparted a measure of His faith to me that enabled me to make the crossing. What a wonderful experience to be able to abide in the light rather than stumbling in the darkness. After I had crossed over the bridge, He told me not to worry or fret about the events of life that I walked while in darkness. The sin, guilt, shame, and worldly satisfaction was erased by His shed blood. So today as I am blessed to walk in His light, I do not have the desire for the things I left behind by crossing over the bridge provided by Jesus. Thank you Jesus, for your vivid reminder today, as I walk and fellowship with You and our Father.

The Least of These

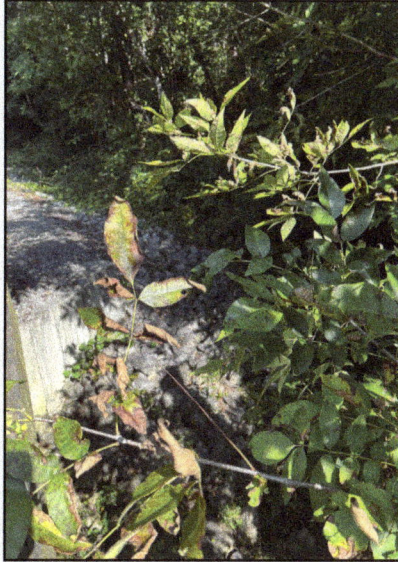

While on a morning walk, I had my attention turned to a sight that I'm sure is overlooked by the multitudes. I really was not searching for anything to write, but was actually tuned in to a selection of hymns that I normally love to hear while walking. As I was returning home, I stumbled upon a sight that was indescribable. I noticed a movement to my right as I crossed the familiar bridge I cross almost daily. A small, unattractive branch attracted my focus. Like me, it was showing its age, as deterioration had set in and brown tinges began to appear. The strange part was that the little branch was waving excitedly from left to right, as if trying to get my attention. It became even more strange as I realized the rest of the branches on the tree were motionless. It was as if I was the last chance for the little branch to get someone to stop and spend a few minutes. I walked on but I could not get the little branch off my mind;

so I returned to the bridge to observe the branch again. I stood waiting for several minutes hoping it would wave again, but the wave never returned. I began to question why this happened and how could it happen?

As I stood gazing at the branch, my thoughts were enhanced to the point of the branch having my attention and desiring to relate a story to me. He started by expressing his appreciation for my stopping and spending a few moments with him. He related that he didn't have much time left in this season of his life, and he wanted to witness for his Creator. He described his life as one of being unnoticed, as if hidden from the majority of those who passed by him. He then began to describe his life as one of surrender, where he received his necessities from the life flowing from within the tree. He related how happy he was to be abiding in another for his strength and sustenance. He seemed so happy to be giving credit to the source of life received from another, to be the witness of his Creator, who placed him in this situation to live his life. As I departed his presence, I thanked him for his testimony and related the pleasure I had received from his dedication.

As I continued my walk, I had an uplifting feeling and a resolve to always consider "the least of these," a phrase from Matthew 25:40. I am so grateful for this unusual meeting with an insignificant-looking little branch with a big heart and a wonderful testimony of our Creator. Colossians 3:3 states, "For ye are dead, and your life is hidden with Christ in God." How important it is that His life is revealed, and my old life does not surface, so He may receive glory and honor as I depend on Him. What a wonderful meeting I experienced with the little branch. What a wonderful story the Holy Spirit imparted to me. I am ever grateful for the pleasure I receive as I encounter lessons of life on my journey of life.

Face of an Angel

Recently I photographed a small waterfall in the midst of a mountain stream. Later, as I was reviewing my photos of the day, I noticed something unusual. I could see what appeared to be a face present as the stream journeyed over the rock-laden terrain. I have shown this photo to several people, and received various explanations and ideas of what appears. I shared it with a friend who wanted to share it with her dear mother, also my friend, who resides in a nursing home. I sent the picture and she shared it with her mother, who said she saw the face of an angel. I realized at the beginning the apparent spiritual nature of the image in the photo, thus the name of this writing was created by my friend's mother. As I continued to study the picture, I wondered if this could be an angel of which I was unaware. The image definitely resembled my idea of the raiment an angel or a spiritual saint may adorn.

As I further pondered the photo, I saw a spiritual person on his Christian walk like we as believers travel. 1 John 1:7 says, "But if we walk in the light, as He is in the light, we have fellowship one with another, and the blood of Jesus cleanses us from all sin." The image appears to be rising from the crimson stream that flows from Calvary, freshly cleansed by the blood of Jesus. He had been convicted of a sin, confessed his sin and now is rising to continue his walk in the light. If you notice, the light is shining on his head revealing fellowship with the Farther and the Son is restored. Now he can continue his journey toward the mark of the high calling illuminated by the light of Jesus.

I thank my Father that Jesus is my all in all. He can appear in various ways to proclaim His love for me. On this day I was so blessed to be reminded of His constant presence with me as He used this image to call my attention to these truths that brighten the path I walk with Him. May He receive glory in all things.

There Will be Showers of Blessings

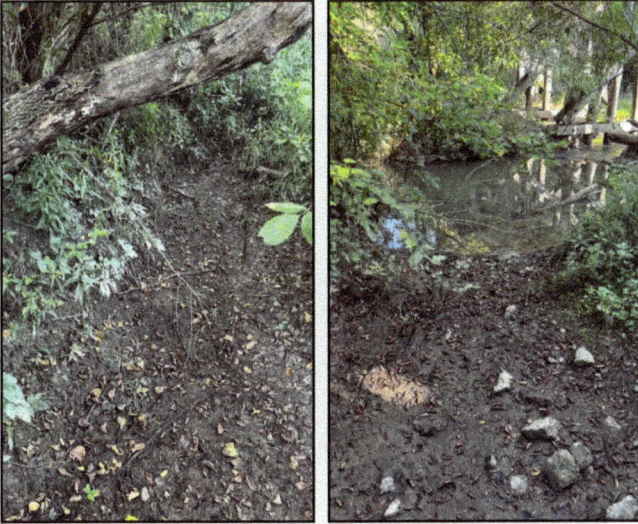

As I walked today I noticed the creek bed I viewed from the bridge above was completely dry. The dryness seemed be caused by the recent lack of rain. The level of the creek in the foreground was lower than usual and thus unable to supply water for this small tributary.

As I became aware of the dryness present, I began to wonder how the dryness affected the little stream. Was there sadness experienced? Was there any hope in the future? Would life return to normal again? Did it wonder if it was at fault? Or, what should I be thinking? These are a few questions I considered maybe the creek bed was musing.

As I related this scene to my life, I recalled my own periods of dryness. In those periods, I'm sure I posed similar questions as to the cause or purpose of such a season. I have learned as I have gone through these periods that they don't last forever and a lesson is to be learned. In these times I have experienced all of the questions the creek bed wondered about.

I have discovered that my Father allows me to experience theses times to mature me into the son He desires me to be. I know I have probably tried to answer the questions on my own, without being satisfied. When I eventually realize who my Father is and who I am to Him, I am made aware that He desires my dependence on Him. In times like these I have found that showers of blessings always arrive and the circumstances wane as my thoughts return to the goodness of my Father. His love for me always washes away the dryness and lessons learned enable me to remember His love and presence with me, allowing me to flow once again in fellowship with Him. Yes, the showers of blessings always show up in my deepest moments of need.

Trinity Reminder

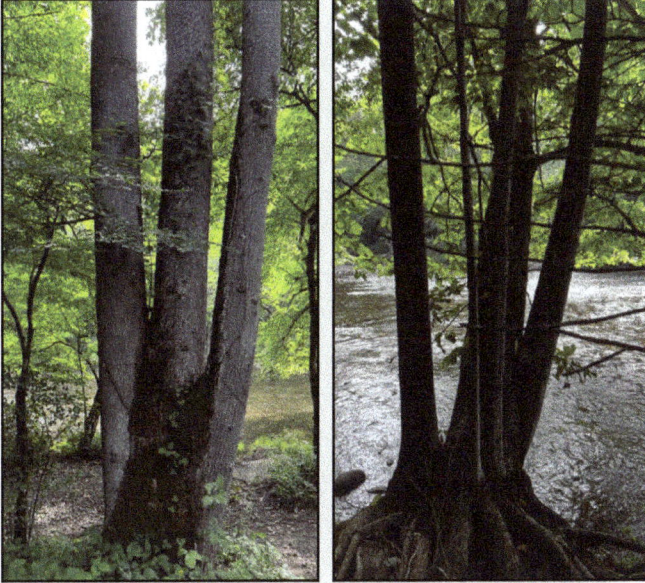

R ecently while hiking a mountain trail, I noticed this tree that reminded me of the Trinity. In the first photo I noticed there were three distinct parts of this tree, yet it was one tree. I then envisioned the three parts sharing a love relationship that had lasted from eternity past as they enjoyed the peaceful flowing of the river of life flowing nearby. My thoughts then wondered if this was a similar setting in which the Father announced His plan to have more children in His Family? His plan would include sending His only begotten Son to die as a payment for the sins of mankind, and to be in union with all who believed. The Son willingly and with great love obeyed the Father, making the Father's plan happen. This union would satisfy the Father's requirement for sin and insure a loving relationship with man. Jesus' imparted divine nature would enable man to lovingly fellowship with the Father. What a great sacrifice the Father made to birth and adopt me into His family.

The second photo shows the result of the Father's plan to have more children in His house. I noticed the Trinity present with more children rejoicing together as a result of the Father's sacrificial love. I also witnessed that now they are all one, fulfilling His desire that we may all be united as one.

What a beautiful reminder of a wonderful Father, Son, and Holy Spirit as portrayed in nature. I am so thankful for the constant reminders of the Father's presence and love as I daily walk His path of life.

About the Author
Ray Brown

After receiving a degree in Pharmacy, Ray practiced his profession in a community setting for 49 years. Having made a decision early in life to follow Christ, Ray has been actively serving in church leadership and teaching roles for many years. His passion is to live a life that reflects what he writes and believes, and to learn to see Christ in everything. Ray and his wife, Ethel, live in Alcoa, Tennessee. They are blessed to be the parents of three grown children, and have eight grandchildren. They are members of Fellowship Church in Knoxville, Tennessee.

Ray Brown

www.ingramcontent.com/pod-product-compliance
Lightning Source LLC
Chambersburg PA
CBHW052117030426
42335CB00025B/3031